FLIGHT OF
THE STORM PETREL

FLIGHT OF THE STORM PETREL

RONALD M. LOCKLEY, 1903-
Illustrated by Noel W. Cusa

DAVID & CHARLES
Newton Abbot   London

PAUL S. ERIKSSON, *PUBLISHER*
Middlebury, Vermont

Frontispiece British storm petrels at night over Skokholm

British Library Cataloguing in Publication Data

Lockley, R. M.
Flight of the storm petrel
  1. Petrels
  I. Title   II. Cusa, Noel W.
  598.4'2   QL696.P6

  ISBN 0-7153-8219-5

Library of Congress Cataloging in Publication Data

Lockley, R. M. (Ronald Mathias), 1903–
  Flight of the storm petrel.

  Bibliography: p.
  Includes index.
  1. Hydrobatidae.   I. Title.
  QL696.P64L63 1983   598.4'2   82-18361
  ISBN 0-8397-2312-1

printed in Great Britain
by R. J. Acford, Chichester
for David & Charles (Publishers) Limited
Brunel House   Newton Abbot   Devon

First published in the United States of America 1983 by
Paul S. Eriksson, *Publisher*
Middlebury, Vermont 05753

Contents

Introduction

For a little while the dark unknown bird with the glittering sepia-black eye lay in my hand passively. No doubt it was temporarily dazed on being dragged into the sunlight from its nesting crevice in the hedge-wall. Roaming the lonely island on that summer holiday I had heard its subdued singing as a mysterious far-off stridulation, musical but in a lower key than a grasshopper's churring. Eagerly approaching the sound, I put my ear to the hoary lichened stones, neatly arranged in a herring-bone pattern, which supported the metre-wide earthen bank. Nearer, the sound was surprisingly loud, a continuous vibrating purr.

A musky odour filled my nostrils as, in my excitement, I worked loose the nearest slanted stone behind which I had glimpsed a sooty black body with a prominent ebony beak and grey-tinged head. The little bird ceased to purr as it retreated to the back of the crevice, exposing a small white egg in a slight depression in the dry earth.

It was not difficult to insert my arm to elbow distance and gently imprison the bird in my half-closed fist, carefully covering its wings to prevent flapping, but allowing its long thin legs and webbed feet to dangle free and helpless. When I drew it forth it spat a little shower of transparent oily fluid on my other hand. This was the source of that musky smell pervading the nest site.

What a delicate, dainty, almost ethereal creature! Hardly larger than a sparrow, but elegantly built with longer wings, and weighing just one ounce (under 30 grams), it seemed almost weightless, far too fragile to ride out storms at sea. Yet this morsel of life in my hand was the original 'stormy petrel' known of old to mariners as Mother Carey's Chicken. To science it is *Hydrobates pelagicus* ('the oceanic water-walker'), originally named from the Greek by Linnaeus, in 1758.

There is an old belief, its origin lost in antiquity but still held by sailors I have talked with, that Mother Carey's Chickens flock closely around ships at sea chiefly (some say only) in rough weather. Superstitious persons feared to see them then, as it was believed that Mother Carey was some sort of satanic sea-witch—evidently possessing the key to Davy Jones' locker, that submarine mortuary where drowned persons are said to repose at first. Her Chickens assembled close to ships in distress from gales, awaiting the drowning of sailors, whose souls Mother Carey had the power to turn into stormy petrels. Only prayer could save them in such danger, but the damned souls of those wicked men and mariners who ill-treated their fellows—mutineers, pirates and such bad company—were condemned to inhabit the bodies of stormy petrels wandering forever without rest upon the restless ocean.

That is one superstition. A happier and more plausible belief is that the name is a corruption of *Mater Cara*—the Mother Beloved, Our Lady. When these little birds appeared beside a ship before a severe storm began it was regarded as a signal to the faithful that the Virgin Mary, while warning them to prepare for the gale, would answer their prayers with her protection and care. The word 'petrel' also has a religious connotation: it is a diminutive of Peter (peter-el, formed no doubt in the same way as 'cockerel' and 'dotterel'), and arose from the storm petrel's habit of walking, or appearing to walk, on the surface of the sea, pattering with its webbed feet as it flits along. St Peter, it will be remembered, walked (somewhat fearfully) on the stormy sea of Galilee at Christ's invitation (Matthew, *14, 29*). A similar derivation applies to one of the vernacular names of the white-faced storm petrel (*Pelagodroma marina*), known sometimes as the J. C. bird in New Zealand where it is the most common of storm petrels. It has long legs and large feet, and its water-walking habit seems at times more pronounced than that of *Hydrobates*.

Possibly 'storm' or 'stormy' was attached to this group of birds, at least in Britain, because the two storm petrels most common in British waters, *Hydrobates pelagicus* and *Oceanodroma leucorhoa*, Leach's storm petrel, are frequently swept inland during gales and are found exhausted far from the sea, truly 'stormy' petrels. This happens most often to young birds taking wing for the first time in autumn and caught in equinoctial gales. But the adjective is more likely to have resulted from the belief of sailors that storm petrels appear about ships more frequently before and during storms than in calm weather, and are regarded on that account as portents of bad weather. Storm petrels can indeed be seen feeding at sea near ships during good weather but they are perhaps more easily overlooked then. It is a fact that strong winds seem to give them greater confidence to follow within a few metres of a ship's stern. For example, off the lonely pinnacle of Rockall, some 250 kilometres west of the Outer Hebrides, when the Fleetwood trawler (from which Stephen Marchant and I had hoped to land on this isolated stack—but bad weather prevented us) was labouring and lurching alarmingly in a Force 10 hurricane—the worst I have ever experienced at sea—we watched dozens of storm petrels flutter confidently under the ship's plunging stern.

It was wonderful and astonishing to realise that these tiny birds were perfectly at ease in the raging wind which blew clouds of spray from the confused tops of the waves. Always keeping close to the water, at one moment they pattered with webbed feet lightly touching the surface, swaying wings in full control of the body in these feeding movements; in the next instant the head would dip down to snatch up minute items invisible to us. Frequently a bird would half or wholly submerge to seize food which the ceaseless heaving of the water had exposed but immediately enveloped. Each time they emerged, their wings were already open, the oily plumage instantly repelling every drop of water.

They took advantage of the momentary shelter afforded by the trough of each swell or wave; then, riding or wind-borne close upon the windy crest, made use of its airlift for the next downward plunge. The magic of that graceful, easy, ceaseless flight over the stormy sea has remained; and Stephen and I understood so much better how this petrel can survive the gales it must encounter in the open ocean. Much of the time is spent flying in slow wind eddies found in the troughs, sheltered by the tall crests of the rolling swell.

Then, more than fifty years ago, almost nothing was known about the lives of the storm petrels of the world, which are the smallest of all sea birds. It was all the more exciting to discover *Hydrobates* breeding on the remote abandoned island of Skokholm, off Pembrokeshire in Wales. Friend Harry and I were once more on summer holiday, on my part inspired by a secret dream of boyhood that I might find a small island where I could dwell alone with nature, with the birds and wild flowers which had long been my passion. I had abandoned hopes of the academic career my parents had planned for me, and had rented a small farm in a Monmouthshire valley—a little too near the industrial march of Cardiff for my liking. Neighbour Harry, artist and country-lover, more than twice my age, was ever ready to escape from the monotony of his business as dentist in that city. We would start off in his car, camping at some remote spot in the Welsh mountains before reaching the western sea. In the previous summer we had enjoyed a brief but exciting visit to the 300 hectare island of Skomer, off the south-west coast of Pembrokeshire (part of the former Welsh princedom of Dyfed—its restored name today). Skomer was rich with thousands of nesting shearwaters, puffins, auks and gulls, but we encountered no storm petrels. At one time it had been farmed, but now its fields were full of bluebells and bracken; only its old farmhouse was occupied, by a small family living there chiefly for health reasons. It had a sheltered haven and was easy to reach from the nearest mainland boat-beach.

A few miles south of Skomer lies the smaller red sandstone island of

Skokholm, about 100 hectares, isolated in the open Atlantic. We had tried to sail there, but it had been surrounded by the white leaping swell of a westerly gale which prohibited landing on its harbourless coast. Local fishermen told us that it had not been farmed for many decades, the house was derelict, the land given up to 'swarms of rabbits, thousands of cocklollies [shearwaters] and millions of puffins'. Through binoculars on that June day it looked tantalisingly beautiful: sheets of bright pink armeria (thrift), acres of ultramarine bluebells, and a white edge of sea-campion above glowing red, almost purple, sandstone cliffs.

But a year had to pass before Harry and I were able to cross to Skokholm on our next Whitsuntide holiday. Even then we had to wait impatiently for two days while a gale died away, camping in view of the island but enjoying the vivid wildlife of the mainland cliffs, finding nests of raven, chough and peregrine. It was not wasted time, for a new hope had suddenly sprung up in my heart. Jim, one of the fishermen who had agreed to ferry us across to the island, proved to be the nephew of the absentee tenant, whom he called Bulldog Edwards (to distinguish him from others of the numerous Edwards tribe inhabiting the Marloes peninsula). Jim had told us casually that his uncle was now too old to be much interested in the island; he had farmed it as a young man, but had abandoned it when his wife had died, and retained the lease only in order to continue to employ a contractor to catch the rabbits for him each winter—sometimes Jim agreed to catch them. Bulldog lived on the mainland—why not go and see him?

In an earlier book (*The Island*), I have described how I obtained the lease of Skokholm, and went to live there, enjoying the good fortune to buy for a song a wooden topsail schooner, wrecked there soon after I settled in, which provided much of the material to repair the little farmhouse. Since that wondrous time—for a young man escaping into happiness in contact with the sea and the clean sky, every sense alert to enjoy the wished-for Crusoe life, alone and solaced by the beauty of nature, listening to the music of the birds and curious to uncover the story of their mysterious lives—I have studied other storm petrels on other small islands of the world. In particular Leach's and Madeiran fork-tailed petrels breeding on certain northern hemisphere islands; and Wilson's and white-faced storm petrels in New Zealand and Antarctic seas.

In twelve years living at Skokholm up to the outbreak of war those early studies had established the strange facts about the breeding habits of both storm petrel and Manx shearwater, two members of the tubenose order or Procellariiformes. These proved to be typical of that order, as subsequently revealed by the painstaking studies of later observers.

My wife and daughter and I were obliged to leave Skokholm for the duration of the war, and we did not go back to live there permanently afterwards. In 1946 we reopened the bird observatory we had established there in 1933 (originally because we were glad to welcome the many volunteers who wished to help with our sea and migrant bird marking work) which has ever since been managed by the West Wales Naturalists' Trust. But the studies have gone on steadily, under a succession of young wardens who, as I had at the same age, desired to live close to nature—and find themselves, for the experience is a good lesson in self-reliance—in this vivid island environment, shut away from the worries and problems of mainland existence.

It is from this wealth of knowledge—still being gathered—that this present book is written. I acknowledge with pleasure the studies of storm petrels by other observers, and shall refer to them as necessary in my narrative. But I do not intend to reproduce here the numerous graphs, scientific formulae, and somewhat too teleological (some verge on the tautological) descriptions with which some of their papers are encumbered. In this book I wish instead to try to recapture in plain language that first fine careless rapture of discovering, or uncovering, day by day, month by month, year by year, the intimate details of the life-history of the species which make up the world total of a score of true storm petrels.

Fortunately the early record was set down each day, in the diaries which I have kept since boyhood. Some of the rapture is also recorded there, not always in poetic words, but discernible in the brief scribbled descriptions, and not seldom an exclamation mark—that symbol which in a single stroke tells the recorder so much more than he has found time to set down in prosaic words. The reader of this book may be troubled now and then by a certain degree of anthropomorphism, for the lone naturalist is apt to put human thoughts and words into the mind and mouth of any creature he has, by study, grown fond of. But I do not really apologise; perforce we must judge by human values and behaviour, our only yardstick; and animals seem to be almost human at times.

I
Island of the petrels

My diary of 7 to 9 June 1927 records that we were reluctant to leave Skokholm. The weather was perfect, calm and rich in changing colours of light clouds and shadows over the sea, where silver tide-races ran like rivers around the island headlands. We stayed an extra night in order to enjoy again the grand concert of the shearwaters, which came screaming home to their burrows at midnight; but long before dawn all had vanished, save the skins of a few freshly killed unlucky birds—evidence of predation by the gulls which nest abundantly over the whole island.

In the black night bedlam of the cocklollies it was easy to overlook the faint purring of the storm petrels, and at first we did not realise that they too had a homing inflight from the sea. Standing close to the hedge-wall where we had first found one in its crevice, we could hear several purring from other holes along the walls which divide up the little fields, now much overgrown with heather and bracken, at the eastern end of Skokholm. We at last realised that the faint squeaking reply floating around our heads came from petrels which seemed to be chasing or circling each other. Possibly a courtship dance, or a territorial pursuit? The white rump was all that human eyes could see in the darkness. Was its significance for just such an activity? Like the white scut of the running rabbit was it a 'follow-me' sign for recognition in darkness or subdued light?

Skokholm, Irish Sea breeding ground of the British storm petrel

Lapwings

Dawn seemed to come with incredible swiftness. Just two dark hours, and we suddenly realised that the night birds had vanished. The soft-winged storm petrels had melted away unseen. Shearwaters no longer blundered into us, or (since we were the trespassers) we into them, as they left their burrows for the sea. Once a petrel had brushed against my face, as light as a big moth. When the sun rose Harry lay down in the heather and was soon fast asleep. But I was too excited by thoughts and plans for coming to live at Skokholm—if only I could secure the lease, perhaps even buy the island? But I had no money. However, the lease-rent was within my means—in fact very modest—only £25 a year, evidently because today nobody was willing to live here permanently? How absurd—it was the most wonderful place I had ever set eyes upon! Basking in the sun, I wrote up my diary, recording the species of birds we had seen. Over thirty, and what was delightful, the number of homely land birds which would be living with me . . . if and when . . . It was nice to think I would not lose some old favourites of my Monmouthshire home: blackbird (I had found one nest of four eggs and the cock was at that moment serenading me from the broken chimney of the cottage), pied wagtail (a family of fledged young, and the old birds nesting again in the garden wall), dunnocks busy in the bracken around, a sedge-warbler singing in the lush vegetation below the well (a fine spring of fresh water flowing there—never failing, the fishermen said).

There was a swallow's nest in the rafters of the large stone-walled barn, under a roof which had a large portion of its heavy stone tiles blown away by

Mallards

winter gales. Stonechats were chatting from the taller clumps of heather, skylarks singing in the sky, meadow pipits in the meadows, rock pipits in pairs along the broken-down rocks around the whole island. Snipe, curlew, lapwing, mallard and moorhen inhabited the wet ground of the central plateau . . . Smoke rose suddenly from the chimney of the cottage, alarming the blackbird into flight. The fishermen were stirring, though it was only 5 a.m. What an odd pair they were! Jim the tall one was as garrulous as a jay; Jack, short, reserved, silent, pleased me more—he was always busy with some useful chore, mending a sail, weaving withies to repair a lobster-pot. The fishermen had developed a routine to make best use of the fine fishing weather: up at five, make a driftwood fire in the broken-down cooking stove, boil the kettle for tea and put on a pot of sea-birds' eggs—half a dozen would be boiled at a time, from which three or four would be considered edible— the rest were 'addled'—contained too large an embryo. No formality of washing-up. They would be away all day to their sixty lobster-pots set in 'strings' of a dozen around the island shore. In the evening they returned to cook their supper—fried sea-bird eggs and home-cured bacon, bread and butter, washed down with mugs of tea. Again no washing-up, the utensils were hung up filthy. They were tired, but before darkness they made a foray across the huge colonies of yodelling gulls on the plateau, and among the rocks where the handsome razorbills were nesting, to collect a fresh supply of eggs.

Some thick driftwood was placed on the hearth and smothered with the accumulated wood-ash in the hope that it would smoulder all night, and be poked into flames for the breakfast cooking. Afterwards both men flung themselves fully dressed (Jack removed his boots, Jim did not) upon a wide plank bed home-made of driftwood. Jack was soon snoring, but as long as we were present Jim talked non-stop.

When the first shearwater came screaming home we left the tired fishermen and joined the night-birds through the hours of darkness, paying more attention to the behaviour of the dainty storm petrels on the last night. They seemed to be nesting everywhere: in the hedge-banks crowned with gardens of tiny flowers—stonecrop, scabious, sheep's sorrel, pearlwort, stag's horn plantain—in crevices in the red cliffs, in holes in the ground among shearwater burrows, even in the broken walls of the house and the outbuildings. But easiest to observe with our hand torches were those which were incubating their single white egg close behind the herring-bone stone face of the old farm hedges. These had been beautifully constructed, probably more than two centuries earlier in the heyday of island farming, to shelter stock and crops. The island was once famous for producing seed corn and butter, Jim informed us, but now decades of encouraging the rabbits to burrow had almost levelled some hedges to the ground, a process accelerated by the rabbit-trapper opening holes for them in these dry banks.

I could not easily see myself as an island farmer restoring those once-neat hedges and fields. I was happy that the birds were in possession. Jim said the cocklollies and puffins (he did not seem to be aware of the existence of the storm petrels) had vastly increased since Bulldog had ceased to live at Skokholm. Every rabbit hole in summer was occupied by these burrowing birds. Not so long ago the local fishermen would set nets in the cliff slopes

Razorbills

overnight to catch the birds, which were used as bait for the lobster-pots. Jim darkly hinted that rival fishermen still set nets for cocklollies and puffins secretly, when he, as custodian appointed by his uncle, was not around. Adding that he wouldn't ever do such a thing himself, it was cruel to the birds, despite the fact that 'them cocklollies be the best bait for shellfish, mind 'ee'. Probably this declaration was specious for our benefit. He knew we were ardent bird-lovers, from our conversation; and once I had reproached him when, walking together across the island in search of gulls' eggs (for we too tried them and found fresh ones very good eating), he squelched with his clogs each nest containing three. Because, he said, the full clutch was likely to be incubated or, as he put it: 'hard-sat, addled I calls it. Thee mus' take only singles or twos. They'm fresh-laid. Them gulls'll lay again, each time thee robs 'em'. But we had seen a trammel net lying in their boat, and some black and white feathers caught in the folds. Later I was to learn from Jack that they had used it to take fish in a tideway, but the same net would be equally effective when set on the cliffs to snare birds flying down to the sea by night. Jim's natural garrulity snared him into prevarications and unnecessary explanations; he wanted to excite our interest, out of his inner loneliness. One could listen to his stories, embroidered or half-truths and mostly hearsay, without the need to believe them. He was a poor restless ragged fisherman who might have been a poet in other circumstances. In his shoes, with his lean upbringing in the remote fishing village, would I not have been just as much in need of exploiting the swarming sea birds of this lonely island? In due course, I was to find that old documents dating back to Norman times mentioned Skokholm's 'farm of the birds' as a profitable asset down the centuries, and rented out to tenants, a special perquisite of living on the island. It was to end with my occupation of Skokholm.

The vast summer population of sea birds had departed by the time I gained possession of my new island kingdom, the lease of which was to start on Michaelmas Day 1927. But there were inevitable delays in disposing of the smallholding, moving west, and in obtaining a suitable boat. As a landlubber I knew nothing about managing a boat in a sea-way. Fortunately I was able to engage the services of the quiet fisherman. Having no home ties, being an orphan and a bachelor, and experienced in serving aboard ketches and schooners, Jack was happy to spend the winter with me. Indeed in my eagerness I would surely have drowned during the stormy period of unusually heavy autumn gales without his wisdom in refusing to allow me to cross to Skokholm in unsuitable weather.

Jack knew the exact limits of risk in sailing the little second-hand open boat I bought on his advice. It was only 16½ft long, but it had to be easy to handle and light enough to be winched well above the storm line in South Haven, the landing place which is no more than a fissure in the cliffs. Neither of us was expert at managing the little engine, which frequently broke down as a result. But Jack had fitted a stout mast and sewn a strong canvas lug sail, and this was our insurance—and I had a new joy in its peacefulness—to be used on all occasions of sufficient wind, if necessary reefed down in bad weather. Then, like the storm petrel, she flew bravely over the rough water and fierce tide-races.

I renamed her *Storm Petrel*.

2

Winter into spring

Great storms shook the coast of Wales throughout much of October, felling trees inland, and making it impossible to stand upright on the cliffs when I crawled there to view my new home majestically veiled in the white foam of enormous Atlantic breakers. It was 21 October before it was calm enough to land my few sticks of furniture and boxes of books on the island. Ten days later we settled in with a further load, including a sack of bread (I was soon baking my own) and tinned provisions to last a few weeks.

The first task was to effect temporary repairs to the roof of the farmhouse, so that we had a dry place in which to sleep. This meant collecting all usable sheets of corrugated iron we could find—long blown off the buildings—nailing them to the half-rotten rafters and placing large stones and planks atop to weigh them down against the gales which followed. The walls of all the farm buildings and of the house at Skokholm were built (or rebuilt) not less than two centuries ago, by the local economical method of that period. No lime mortar or cement was used to hold the stones together during the building, probably because of the difficulty and expense of bringing these materials in quantity from the mainland. Instead fine sifted earth was puddled with water to make mud to bed in the irregular-shaped stones quarried from outcrops of the sandstone rock. Only the outside and exposed top of the wall, with its smoothly plumbed and levelled face of stone, received a waterproof coat of hard mortar, made of lime, sand and coal-ash, filling the interstices between the exposed surface of the outer stones. The old mortar seemed flint-hard, holding the walls upright and firm so long as the top remained impervious to rain. Of course the mud within had quickly dried out, but was retained in place by the outer coat of mortar remaining intact. But during many decades the occasional accident, and sometimes deliberate action by man, had dislodged an outer stone here and there, or a capstone had been knocked off. This provided entry for rain and wind, small birds and other animals, and insects burrowing into the dry mud.

Mice—the house species *Mus musculus*—said to have been accidentally imported with bales of hay or straw early in this century, found these holes in the walls convenient dry cover for living. Normally feeding on a vegetarian diet they multiplied rapidly all summer, spreading over the whole island wherever they could find dry places in which to conceal their nests. The hedge-banks were ideal. In winter they concentrated within the buildings, as we were soon to find, sharing the warmth made by our fire, in the evenings seeking every crumb boldly around our feet. They were a considerable pest; it was necessary to lock up all food in a mouseproof cupboard. But during the cold and gales of winter, when their normal grass and plant food was withered up, they suffered a drastic decline in population, and were rare in the house by the spring.

British storm petrel

We had heard, on that first visit in June, the purring of storm petrels about the house and in the high-banked garden hedge-wall. Now, on 31 October, starting on the repair of the roof, I uncovered a full-grown storm petrel as I lifted a stone near the top of the rear wall of the house. It lay in a recess scratched out of the dried mud in the heart of the wall. Just in time, as it opened its wings, I grabbed and held it. Strange to find one so late in the year! What did it mean? It was nearly five months since Harry and I had seen this charming little bird incubating its solitary egg. Perhaps the petrel was double-brooded, and this was the grown child of a second hatching? From its fresh-looking plumage, with pale grey or whitish edges to some feathers of the wings and back, and its sharp claw tips (in the breeding season the adult claws wear down in burrowing, and scratching against rocks) I was sure it must be a young bird. It was lively, struggling to be free, and in my hand I could feel it was well fleshed, not in the least a sick, ailing relic of the summer season.

'Jack, what shall we do with this storm petrel? Shall we take it down to the sea?' It seemed the kindest thing to do, now that we had destroyed its home in the wall. I wanted to place a ring on its leg to identify it, and had been in correspondence with the founder of the *British Birds* Ringing Scheme, the famous ornithologist H. F. Witherby. He had promised to send me what rings I needed for studying birds at Skokholm, but as yet none had arrived. On the rocky landing steps in South Haven, I opened my hand. The little black object with the white rump fell, evidently slightly dazed, towards the calm water, touched it lightly with its webbed feet, then rose clear and with zigzagging flight headed low over the sea away from the land. For as long as we could keep it in sight—not far, it was so small it merged with the ripples of the distant tideway—it continued to fly. 'Isn't that amazing! If that *is* a young bird, this must be its first flight, perhaps its first stretching of its wings! I had the impression that it had never seen the sea before, was even scared of alighting on it. What do you think, Jack?'

Difficult to get my shy, silent, stoic companion to say anything but his typical polite 'Ah!', acknowledgement that he had heard. But I knew he shared something of my admiration and wonder for this brave dash to freedom by this tiny bird straight from the crevice in which it had been born, by his rare comment of several sentences: 'Ah, it'll surely be back come the spring, sir? Many's the time I seen Mother Carey's Chickens on a stormy day, following our schooner down the Bristol Channel, when I were a deck 'and. Them comes real close to a ship when gales be blowing. A dainty bird, the stormy petrel as 'ee calls it, sir. Aye, stronger on the wing than thee'd 'ave thought possible.'

'I wish you'd drop the "sir", Jack. All men are equal on this island.'

'Aye, aye, sir! Force o' 'abit 'mong seamen, sir.'

On the next day, 1 November, a strong southerly wind increased to a full gale. As I resumed the repair of the roof I wondered greatly if the little petrel I had taken from the wall could survive such a fierce onshore wind. Would it be blown far inland—the fate of many young sea birds weak on the wing? No good worrying too much. Rebuilding that wall, I deliberately left a space for the storm petrel to return to nest there. Secure at last on my island, I was not in the least dismayed by the ensuing month of wild weather. I was too preoccupied in making a shelter and home for the future. The little house had been wisely built, facing the mainland, but tucked away behind a rock outcrop that protected it from the prevailing south-west wind. And here too came for shelter many land birds, to amuse me.

When at last the wind veered to east it brought a wintry coolness, frost inland, and a calming sea. There was beauty in this sudden change, which brought flocks of migrating birds from the misty land horizon to settle for a while on our warmer, frost-free island. We hastened to make the best use of the day to ferry over materials for the repair of the house. It was my birthday, as it happened; my diary records:

Tuesday, 8 November.

I am 24 today, and realising my greatest ambition, which is to live happily on this beautiful island, lonely, set in this silver sea, preparing a home for the dear girl who will come—once I have got a roof on the house and made it habitable by next spring. How little I could have dared hope to live here a few months ago!

As soon as it was light we sailed and motored in *Storm Petrel*, 'on the first of the tide'—as Jack insists we must always try to do—for it is quiet then and flowing north through Jack Sound. A lovely crossing, with 'herring-birds' (as Jack calls them—they are really guillemots in winter plumage without their black collars) diving after sprats in the rippling edge of the current.

We hurried to Trehill Farm where our goods are delivered for the present (until I can build my own depot near the landing-beach—another big task on my list of priorities). We loaded Jim Codd's cart with new windows, door, paint, nails, boxes and bags, etc. and drove the lot the mile distance down to Martinshaven. My boat was too small for such a large cargo, so we filled up Jack's bonny fishing boat *Foxtrot*, 23ft long; and threw in as well a half ton of cement and lime for mortar-making. With some difficulty we launched the laden boat, but presently with a fair north-easterly breeze and a south-going tide we sailed fast for Skokholm. So peaceful without an engine, the sun bursting through, time to sit and stare during the 53 minutes it took to sail to Skokholm steps. A grand morning's work.

The rest of the perfect day passed all too swiftly in unloading and carting everything up to the farmhouse. It took an hour to winch Jack's boat up the Skokholm slipway, probably the longest boat ever hauled ashore here. This double-bowed ex-ship's boat is the apple of Jack's eye (we had sailed in her to the island last June), and he is taking no chances with sudden changes of weather.

Guillemots

The winch is very old, home-made by Bulldog Edwards long ago from the big and little cog-wheels of some old farm machine. I had paid Bulldog £2 for it! I wonder how long it will last?—some of the teeth of the main wheel are almost rusted away.

How beautiful it was on the island today! Flooding with birds, escaping from the cool mainland wind and frost. I saw droves of Starlings, Blackbirds and Thrushes, several Chaffinches, Stonechats, Ravens, a Greenfinch, a Kestrel, a Buzzard, and in North Haven a pair of Choughs making their ringing keep-in-touch cry. Jack saw a Woodcock, and wished he had a gun to make it into a supper for us. They come here in scores, he says, if the cold east wind persists.

Injured snow bunting

There was a poor Bunting unable to fly and in a moribund condition beside the old limekiln near the landing. I did not know what species it was when I brought it indoors, where it expired in spite of our warming it near our driftwood fire. But from the description in Witherby's *Practical Handbook of British Birds* later this evening it proved to be a female *Snow Bunting*, the first I have ever seen of this Arctic species. Where had it been born? Greenland, Iceland, or perhaps nearer, the Cairngorm Mountain corries—the book gives a list of nesting localities.

I wrote a description of this beautiful bird as it lay on the table, in a letter to my sweetheart far away in Monmouthshire—for I owed her a reply to two of hers received today.

The mystery of the long migration performed by this pretty seed-eating bunting troubled my head for a while. Jack lay snoring on his driftwood bed. It was close to midnight. Before turning in upon my truckle-couch in the little side-room, I walked outside to see the stars, and listen. No sound of shearwater or petrel—they were far away somewhere over the ocean? But I could plainly hear the wailing of lapwing, the quacking of duck and—to my great joy—the faint gaggling of wild geese, from the region of the central bog and ponds.

Song and Senses

The winter seemed to fly by. According to weather the land birds came stayed awhile, and passed on, some heading west towards Ireland, some south towards Cornwall. The first shearwater returned to repair its burrow and drive out any rabbits there in February; wheatears arrived, inspecting their shallow nest-holes in March; two months in which part of the time I was busy stripping the wonderful unexpected gift of the wreck of the schooner *Alice Williams* (bought for £5 from the underwriters, she was worthless to anyone else) suddenly and immovably broken overnight upon the red cliffs of Skokholm. Abandoned by her crew, near the mainland shore, she had no one aboard. She was to save me hundreds of pounds in timber and fittings I needed for the repair and furnishing of the cottage. Late in March rooks and chiffchaffs passed by, cawing and singing to advertise their transient visit. At noon on 2 April, Jack rushed into the house shouting 'Mr Lockley! Puffins, sir!'

The comical-looking birds had made their first landing while Jack had been painting the *Storm Petrel*, which needed a spruce-up after the hard wear and knocks of the winter crossings, at her berth on the slipway in South Haven. They were sitting peacefully, as if glad to rest, about their burrow entrances on the slopes already white and yellow with the first spring flowers—thick clumps of primroses and tufts of scurvy grass. No doubt to fisherman Jack they were evidence of the renewal of the lobster season; alone with the talkative Jim he would have set nets to catch them for bait. But I like to think that, spending a winter with me, Jack had acquired a less predatory, more protectionist attitude towards the island birds, of which we had talked much during the long evenings alone together. His enthusiasm

Puffins and primroses on Skokholm

was growing with the new knowledge I had tried to impart, and was plain in his excited announcement of the arrival of the first of the 20,000 puffins which at that time spent the summer on the island.

Moreover I had finally persuaded Jack to stay on for the summer, by offering to share the lobster-fishing with him. His last summer's mate had left the district. We would use the *Storm Petrel* to go after Skokholm lobsters, crayfish and crabs every fine day; and in days too rough for fishing, I would pay him for helping me to complete the repairs to the cottage. We had completely restored the old barn, meanwhile, and had moved into it as a temporary home; and it would not be long before the house would be sufficiently mended and habitable—for my marriage planned to take place early in July. I had used up every scrap of my meagre capital in these repairs; and in future would have to find a living from island produce: a good vegetable ga. den (already planted), rabbits, the fishing and a flock of sheep I intended to introduce in the autumn.

Not until 29 April did the first storm petrels return. My diary records that, returning from setting lobster-pots, 'we heard a pair crooning to each other their weird reiterated song from beneath a pile of loose rock near the landing place'. In the middle of May I heard the same song from that space I had left at the top of the wall above my bedroom, so loud that the wall itself seemed to vibrate: 'Urr-rr-rr-rr-rr-rr!' It went on and on, now and then interrupted with a kind of hiccup—'Chikka!' For such a little bird its loudness and persistence is astonishing. But I welcomed my unseen companion in the bedroom wall, pondering the meaning of its serenade until, tired with the day's activities, I fell asleep. A friend, Charles Oldham, who has listened patiently to this song, told me he had once recorded an unbroken run of purring, with eighty-three 'chikkas' inserted. He thought that even the nightjar, which has a similar reeling song on one note, could not equal that! Long ago, as a young man, Oldham and his friend Bertram Lloyd had visited Skokholm, and heard many storm petrels at night. 'They sound to me,' he said whimsically, 'like a fairy being sick!'

What was the meaning of the dancing nocturnal flight of the incoming petrel? It seemed plain that the long purring song of the bird in the nesting crevice was to advertise its presence, to attract a mate. The singer seemed to be vastly excited; and frequently unable to wait until dusk. You could hear the song in the afternoon, even at times in the morning if you made a noise in passing close to the nesting crevice, or if you imitated the purring vocally. As soon as the sun went down in the western sea the evening crescendo began in the hedge-walls, and from the talus of the broken sandstone cliffs. The purring lasted well into July, but was at its height during May and June.

The incoming bird does not purr, but sings a softer note or is silent. It is almost a gentle cackle: 'Kwic-urr' (or 'cuch-ah' as my Highland friend

Seton Gordon preferred to write it), repeated two or three times. It is easier
to see the inflighting birds by moonlight, which does not seem to put them
off, although they seem, in my experience, more numerous on a dark night,
like their large island relatives the shearwaters. These are most noisy on the
blackest night as they scream overhead and home in on their burrows. This
shearwater screaming quite drowns the softer songs of the storm petrel; it
puzzled me at first, because although the little petrel seemed to be calling
from the nesting crevice to its mate, the shearwater already in its burrow was
usually silent—it was the incoming shearwater which roared out its amazing
guttural strangulated cock-crow on the wing.

It is possible that the louder crying of the incoming shearwater on the
darkest night is partly to echo-locate its burrow—to receive back from
the configuration of the ground (earth or rock) the familiar echoes of its own
voice, which vary in pitch with the nearness and contours of the ground. In
the labyrinthine rocks of the Berlengas Islands off Portugal even I could
detect at night the different pitch of the echoes of shearwater voices as they
sought their homes in caves and underground fissures. It is now well known
that like certain bats, some birds (oil birds of Central America, edible
swiftlets in Malaysia) find their way in total darkness to nests in caves and
rock chimneys by the use of this sonar.

But our storm petrel returning from the sea is often silent, or soft-voiced
as it circles above its nesting site. If it is the partner of a mate already singing
in the nest-site, it is not necessary for it to, and it probably does not, reply
when flying home. The purring song from the ground is sufficient guidance,
and after a few swift turns in the air above the entrance to the crevice, it
quickly settles, pitching within a few centimetres of the hole, taking a second
or two to fold its long wide wings, then disappearing below. You may hear
the pair squeak together very softly for a while, but no long purring follows,
just short bursts—or silence. Circling in the night air must be principally to
locate the burrow site, just as the diurnal bee circles a few times above its
hive to locate it from memory on returning; and when leaving the bee
likewise circles, this time to imprint the visual location once more (or for the
first time) upon its memory. May the adult petrel, on leaving the nest-
crevice, likewise circle briefly, to imprint the exact location, though it be but
dimly seen in the twilight?

Of course, except in the courtship (pre-egg), incubation and rearing
periods, the incoming bird will have no partner to guide it home by voice. In
that case it must get home by visual or other clues, of which memory may be
important. Just as a musician can play a familiar piece of music from
memory, and man finds his way about his own home confidently in the dark,
by 'muscle memory', that is by brain, hands and feet remembering the
sequence of movements made previously, the petrel, whose sight at night

must be infinitely superior to that of man, automatically makes the necessary well-remembered and correct flight approaches to locate its home. As we shall discuss later, for a young petrel training in locating a future home begins from the moment it first leaves its dark birthplace.

Sometimes, lying in the grass and looking at the sky, watching the late evening inflight of the petrels around midsummer, I would follow the flight of a single lone bird circling round and round, silhouetted within a few metres of my head. After many turns of this aerial dance it might fly away altogether. Or it might be joined by one or more other petrels, in which case it was hopeless to try to follow the individual—it could only be seen as such clearly against the sky. (Using a torch quickly upset the dance, and the petrels usually vanished or behaved unnaturally.) Obviously these aerial roundabouts (or 'pursuits' as they have been termed), which continue so long through the summer, are an essential part of the breeding cycle, and since so few of those individuals which keep it up on any given night seem to settle on the ground, the participants must be unmated, unoccupied or immature birds. They could include adults which have lost their mate, but the majority—as we shall presently consider—must be non-breeders, adolescents which, like human teenagers, are just visiting, instinctively ready to socialise and to mate, but hesitant and unsure from lack of experience.

Not seldom, where there are half a dozen or more birds in the air above a nesting site, the pace quickens, and faint cries of excitement can be heard as the birds seem to touch each other at intervals in the circling, dipping flight. They appear to perform a figure-of-eight at times, as they keep together within a few metres above the breeding colony. But who is chasing whom? How does the petrel recognise sex in the twilit air? Hardly by sight; in the hand it is usually impossible to tell the difference between male and female; plumage and size are virtually identical. Love, for a species which meets intimately and mates only by night, is but a familiar voice, a presence (and in the petrels a familiar smell) in the darkness. Sight may have some importance for the unmated pair in the twilight aerial case, but can have none for the established mated couple in the dark burrow. They must rely principally on recognising each other's voice, as we humans do, in the darkness. When a stranger entered the nest-crevice of a marked mated pair, during my study, it rarely stayed over the ensuing day unless the owners of the home were away; never if one of the pair was at home, or there was an egg or chick in the nest-scrape.

As to smell, in general most students of the physiology of avian senses believe there is little evidence of a strong olfactory sense in birds. Most species have comparatively small olfactory lobes in the brain, which suggests that they do not follow scent trails for food as many mammal

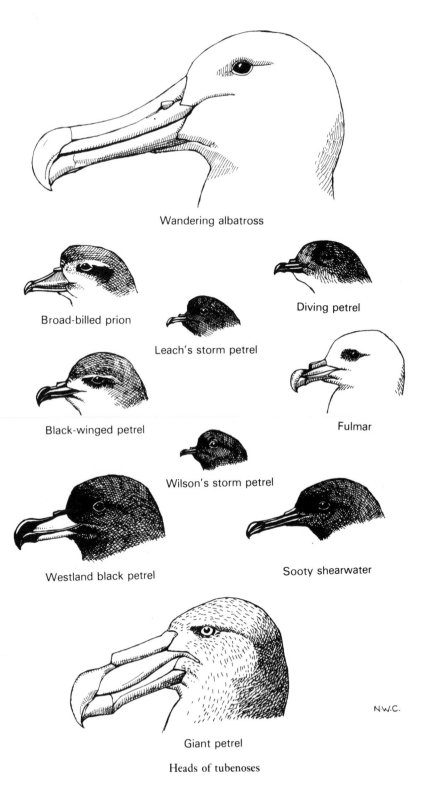

Wandering albatross

Broad-billed prion

Leach's storm petrel

Diving petrel

Black-winged petrel

Fulmar

Wilson's storm petrel

Westland black petrel

Sooty shearwater

Giant petrel

N.W.C.

Heads of tubenoses

species do. However, in the tubenose families the nostrils are large, especially in the storm petrels, and observation and tests have shown that they do have a strong sense of smell. Murphy (1936) wrote that albatrosses and other petrels, and skuas, can detect at sea edible fat, oil, offal, meat and blood. These species appeared rapidly from a horizon apparently empty of birds when strong-smelling fat or oil was trailed behind a ship. In a more recent test Hutchinson and Wenzel of the University of California (1980) observed that storm petrels were among sea birds which concentrated behind a boat experimentally exuding strong-smelling fatty edible oil, but avoided another boat (the control) travelling in the same direction nearby which exuded nothing edible. This trial began purposely at a moment when no bird was visible in the local area of sea; the storm petrels must have scented the food source downwind several kilometres distant.

Storm petrels gather with other sea birds alongside and behind ships during gutting and flensing operations aboard; the larger birds—gulls, albatrosses, shearwaters, skuas, giant petrels—seize the larger portions thrown overboard, while the storm petrels feed more daintily on tiny scraps of flesh and clotted blood floating beyond the squabbling mass of larger scavenging birds. It seems probable from these facts (but is difficult to prove) that the storm petrel may be able to recognise its mate in the darkness of the burrow, not only by voice but by individual scent. Nocturnal mammals such as badgers, hedgehogs and rats and other animals which are active at night, identify the opposite sex or even individuals by scent.

The large nostrils of the storm petrel, united and projecting forward in a single tube conspicuous at the top of the upper mandible, serve other than strictly olfactory functions. In common with many oceanic birds which normally have no access to fresh water, there is a considerable intake of salt when picking up food organisms at sea, far more than the bird needs for health or than it can dispose of through the normal renal excretory system. It accumulates in the form of highly concentrated sodium chloride and associated salts, but is rapidly conveyed in the bloodstream to the network of fine tubes connected with the nasal glands, which discharge it externally in the form of a steady nose-drip. Such birds, swimming at the surface, may be seen to dip their bills as if drinking, but some of the time they are literally wiping or washing their noses of the concentrated salt excretion. When resting on land this salt drip of sea birds is dispersed by a vigorous shake of the head.

Feeding and Fasting

In handling my storm petrels, as previously mentioned, the individual would invariably spit an oily fluid from the opened mouth, and at the same time the nostrils would appear to be smeared with oily material from the same ejection. This habit is common to all tubenoses. The source of this oil has been investigated by several histologists. It is a dietary product which accumulates in the large proventriculus (the much-convoluted stomach). The essential sustaining protein in the food is digested more rapidly than the lipid oils which tend to accumulate here initially; though, like the protein, the oil is eventually metabolised, and converted into body fat (Imber, 1976). Composition of the stomach oil is variable in the different species, but closely related to the oil and fat of many marine animals, including whales and penguins, which feed on zooplankton (especially the shrimp-like krill species), squid and fish rich in the same waxy oils. In retaining stomach oil in the proventriculus for long periods when it is not immediately needed to nourish an already well-fleshed body, the petrel is keeping a reserve of food which will enable it to fast for many days, either when incubating at the nest, or when it cannot feed during bad weather at sea. Even after a fast during incubation at the nest of up to about a week, the storm petrel is still able to eject a quantity of oily fluid at the observer who disturbs it at the nest. Although my adult marked birds were never proved to feed a partner at the nest, surplus stomach oil was evidently now and then squirted forth naturally (that is when undisturbed by me), to hit earth or rock there, leaving a characteristic stain—and that powerful musky odour.

Retaining stomach contents, including the oily secretion from the much-folded walls of the proventriculus, over long periods reaches a record length in some other animals. The male emperor penguin *Aptenodytes forsteri* incubates the single egg for sixty to sixty-five days during the bitterly cold Antarctic midwinter while his mate is away feeding. After laying the egg she has a long walk of perhaps 100 kilometres across the ice to reach the sea, and that distance is increased by the extension of the winter ice shelf by the time she returns fat and full of food. Meanwhile, if the chick hatches before she returns, the male is able to feed the new-born chick with a stomach secretion rich in protein and lipids. Altogether the male loses nearly half his normal pre-breeding weight of around 30 kilograms in a total fasting period of three to four months while living at the breeding colony on the sea-ice, during which he survives by using his large store of body fat. On her return to take over household duties the female does not feed her lean, almost emaciated mate; she reserves the contents of her stomach to dole out food daily to the chick during the somewhat shorter period the male is away, in turn fattening himself and gathering enough food to take back to the growing child.

The larger an animal, the longer it is normally able to fast. This is because its surface area, where loss of body heat is greatest, is small in relation to its bulk or cubic capacity. The largest animals in the world, the baleen whales, after putting on fat by feeding on plankton and fish in high latitudes in summer, need to feed very little during the winter spent in warmer waters while they are engaged in mating, giving birth, and feeding their single offspring. Because of their vast bulk, internal temperatures remain high, and they are believed to fast during the breeding season, for several weeks, even months, like the emperor penguin.

But our storm petrel, although able to put on fat rapidly and store the rich oily product of its food in the proventriculus, has, because of its small body, a relatively large external surface subject to heat loss. Like familiar land birds of the same size, it must surely need to feed much and often, to stay in good condition? As we shall see as our narrative of its life history unfolds, this smallest of sea birds does not indulge a fast of more than a week or so, a period in which nevertheless a fasting sparrow or other small land bird might well die of starvation. But we have already seen that the storm petrel is able to withstand exposure to cold gales and tempestuous waves in temperate latitudes at sea. Even more remarkable is the ability of Wilson's storm petrel nesting amid the snows of Antarctica (page 137) to withstand zero temperatures without incapacitating loss of body heat. But in these petrels, as in the truly Antarctic penguins, the plumage is so thick and densely layered, trapping the body-heated air, that hardly any cold air, and no water, can penetrate to the skin. Water rolls off the oil-preened feathers, while snow does not melt when it alights upon penguin or petrel plumage if the ambient temperature is below zero.

3
Summer days

Those early island years were sweet to live, and good to look back upon today by a perusal of diaries. They were full of the happiness of living in such a vivid, wild yet intensely beautiful environment; and at the same time winning health and new strength from satisfying physical toil. The many pleasant island tasks included growing food in the restored garden, and an extra patch to produce vegetables suitable for the large Chinchilla rabbit warren my wife and I were trying to build up in the expectation of large financial returns from the sale of pelts. This latter enterprise was to prove a failure chiefly because of falling markets, but it was an interesting experiment while it lasted. Then the lobster-fishing with partner Jack in the first two summers was a new delight to me, spending each fine day lifting and dropping our home-made withy cages around the island coast in the most favourable 'holes', known from experience by Jack to yield the best catches of crabs, crayfish and lobsters. Yet it was a period—1928–30—of

Bottle-nosed dolphins

worldwide depression, and often, when we took the weekly catch by boat to
the market at Milford Haven, the returns barely exceeded expenses. I
reaped a richer and more lasting harvest in our encounters with passing
dolphins, pilot whales, seals and innumerable sea birds, as day after summer
day we worked our pots along the island's vivid red sandstone shore.

There was not a moment to spare to be idle. I had marked a dozen nests of
storm petrels in the old hedge-walls, in order to begin a serious study of this
mysterious twilight visitor, which came home so suddenly and swiftly in the
darkness, and was almost never seen by day close inshore when we were
fishing. So long as it was light they were far away, out there somewhere in
the wide ocean. Then one night (1 August), spent fishing until after
midnight, my diary records that 'storm petrels were suddenly over the water
all along the shore in the moonlight'.

Unfortunately, the series of nests I had marked in the summers of
1929–30 were deserted one by one by the mated and ringed pair, owing to
the excessive wariness of the storm petrel. I was to learn that after one, or at
most two, handlings of an adult at the nest, initially to band it with a
Witherby numbered leg-ring, that individual might not be found at the nest
site again, even when the egg was present and incubation well advanced.
The same nervousness and desertion occurred after handling its mate.
Perhaps a visit might be paid to resume incubation of the egg a week or two
later; but as it had remained cold so long, the embryo was too chilled to
survive. In these disturbed nests, if I visited them at night, my torch
sometimes revealed an adult present, but the light scared the occupant, and
it had gone by the morning. This was disheartening, but taught me a lesson.
I was too preoccupied at that time to worry much, except that the physical
work of getting a living, of fishing, and of routine island and boat
maintenance was delaying the serious scientific studies of sea birds which I
had optimistically planned to spend much time upon. But at least I was
having some success in observing a series of marked shearwaters breeding in
shallow burrows a few yards from our back door.

Puffinus puffinus is a much larger bird and a more phlegmatic character,
and, living in its comfortable earthen burrow, if handled gently but firmly,
objected little when lifted up and its ring-number identity was checked. For
ten years from 1929 onwards this colony was to provide me with the material
for a monograph on the Manx shearwater (1942). Still, even the shearwaters
fought shy of too frequent handling at the nest, and one or two deserted at a
critical stage. Then, when I discovered that each partner incubated in shifts
of several days, while the other was away feeding at sea, I hit upon a solution
which avoided perhaps half these inspections, which so troubled the
brooding bird. I placed matchsticks or short dry stalks of dead bracken
(plenty of it around) upright in the entrance to each burrow under

Manx shearwater

observation. If a bird left at any time it easily brushed the feeble barrier
outwards. If it entered a burrow it flattened the sticks *inwards*. Occasionally
the shearwater would pick up one or two of these little sticks and carry them
to the nest—not so much with the intention of lining the nest but as a
'displacement' activity, I believe, as a man absentmindedly plucks and
chews a grass stem to relieve inner tension.

This technique was applied to ten marked nests of the storm petrel under
study at Skokholm in 1931. Some of these had no earth at the entrance, the
birds entered by narrow slits in the slanted stone hedge-wall; in these cases it
was easy to wedge a slight lattice-work of dry stems across the entrance, light
enough to be brushed aside by the bird entering or leaving. Moreover I
selected in this year more convenient nests, in which the incubating bird was
clearly visible as it sat on the egg at the end of a shorter passage, within about
2ft (60cm) of my nose and eye placed close to the entrance. Instead of
pulling out the intervening stone and disturbing both the nest-scrape and
the contour of the wall, I used a suitable length of pliable tying wire, with
one end turned back about 15mm to form a miniature shepherd's crook. By
hooking with this one leg of the petrel just above the bulge of the tarsus
where the feathers begin, it was possible to draw the bird by a steady gentle
pull into the hand.

It was examined as expeditiously as possible, and if not already leg-
banded was marked and returned through the entrance. It immediately
scrambled back to the undisturbed nest-scrape and egg. It was best as far as

possible to make the round of these nests as early as possible in the morning, so that where a bird had been handled, it would have plenty of time to settle down before nightfall activity began. Perhaps the handled bird, which might be found fast asleep on the nest later in the day, regarded the intrusion and ignominious dragging forth into the light of day as just a bad dream? At least this reduction of handling and nest disturbance had fruitful results. Out of the ten marked nests, six young birds developed to maturity and successfully departed on their unknown transocean voyages.

It is from these first studies of banded individuals that the life-history of the storm petrel is unfolded in this book. But I must repeat that I owe a debt to later observers who followed the same techniques, and for a while came to live as appointed wardens at Skokholm Bird Observatory, and carried on the study. Peter Davis was the first of these. In three years, 1954–6, he obtained precise data from thirty-two nests on the incubation and fledging periods (Davis, 1957), which confirmed and amplified my own more modest pioneer study published in 1932. I have freely drawn on the published information on the life-history of this storm petrel by this conscientious observer, a man after my own heart who has continued, since leaving Skokholm, to study birds and other animals on Fair Isle and other remote wild places.

The storm petrel is one of the latest of sea birds to lay its egg. The earliest date in my records has been 2 June; and latest, 6 July. Peter Davis records his earliest as 8 June, and latest as 4 July. But there is a considerable period between the first appearance of a breeding bird at the nest and the laying of the egg. This has been variously termed the courtship, pre-egg, mating or honeymoon period. To be on the safe side most observers call it the pre-egg stage. In Davis's marked nests the average duration of this period was 46.8 ($\pm$9.1) days.

Why such a long gap between arrival, and the production of the egg? To say that animal periodicity is governed by a timing mechanism within the brain which, as one scientist has put it, acts 'as a continuously consulted clock' to inform it automatically what to do next, both diurnally and seasonally, is a far from satisfactory answer.

In order to survive and thrive every species must feed and reproduce. In simplest terms all birds and animals, including man, survive by two sorts of behaviour: the so-called instinctive or innate, and the behaviour which is learned by experience. At birth the human child instinctively seeks the nipple of the maternal breast which it is too blind to see clearly; the newly hatched bird seeks warmth and food in the same unthinking way— instinctively—but is able to learn far more quickly than the human child. Within a few weeks or months, while the child is still a suckling infant hardly able to recognise its parents, the bird has become a completely independent full-grown adult. To achieve this point in its life and survive, it has had to supplement instinctive behaviour with a degree of learning, from experience and association with others of its species, at a speed that is astonishing, but is essential to enable it to find the right kind of food quickly and to avoid being killed by its predators.

The student of birds is baffled by the many extraordinary skills which birds and animals may have, which cannot be 'learned' but must be 'innate'. As when certain species such as the chaffinch, the weaver and bower birds, make their exquisitely and intricately woven nests without having had the opportunity to observe the adults at work on nest-making. The only explanation of this ability, which is also applicable to the skill of wasps, bees and other humble insects in building elaborate nests without the guidance of the adult, is that the animal is born with the 'knowledge' of how to behave so cleverly. Only it is not cleverness or even intelligence; the tiny brain of the wasp which builds an elaborate paper hive, or the much larger brain of the weaver bird which is able to construct a complicated hanging nest with a dummy entrance to deflect and deceive predators, but with a cloth door which it is able to close when it enters or leaves—these skills, which man can never achieve with his own hands, are regarded by most ethologists (students of animal behaviour) as purely innate. The 'information' or key plan on procedure (they say) is inherited in the genes it is born with; the construction of such nests is automatic, a set sequence of actions inspired by a mysterious 'internal drive', including the seasonal sexual urge. The brain of bird and insect holds 'a computer which controls behaviour, producing actions in an orderly manner which enable the subject to survive and reproduce'.

A century ago there was much more belief that these wonders and mysteries of nature were attributable to God, the Deity of Dante who 'moves the sun and the other stars'. It was with some such mixture of common curiosity, puzzlement and perhaps divine awe, that I approached the study of my storm petrels so mysteriously returned from the vastness of ocean to their humble crevices in the island hedge-walls. Walls so beautifully and romantically built—to my thinking—by the sea-captains, their farming sons and labourers; those long-departed men of old who must (as I so often did) have gazed and pondered on the majesty of this sub-ocean environment and its changing moods of calm and storm. 'Enough of speculation!' I would sometimes cry, 'let these darling little birds be, as I am, a complex of internal instinct stimulated by external pressures and experiences giving rise to wisdom or learned behaviour. My main task shall be simply to seek out the truth of their strange way of life.'

The Brood Patch

Nevertheless my admiration and scientific curiosity remained, driving me to meddle with and record their affairs, but more circumspectly now. As soon as I examined and handled the first adults as they appeared in May, I noticed that each had a bald patch in varying stages of defeathering just to the rear of the breast-bone. This bareness, essential to raising the temperature of the egg to body heat, is due to the temporary moulting of the body feathers and underlying down, both short but dense on the lower belly; and is induced, it is believed, by hormonal changes in the metabolism of the breeding adult. A few bird species do not develop brood patches—such as the gannet and cormorant, which incubate by placing their warm feet above the egg or eggs. Some develop more than one—gulls have three separate bare patches to accommodate the three eggs of their normal clutch. In a few species only the male develops a brood patch; he carries out incubation entirely on his own. In the kiwi the female has no brood patch, she is exhausted by laying her enormous egg, and needs to recuperate for many days after. In the phalarope the female, more gorgeously plumaged than the male, is polyandrous—she seeks a male, lays a first clutch, and then mates again with a second male, lays another clutch, and deserts once more.

Pair Formation

Our storm-petrel pair were to remain constant to each other; each spring most of my marked birds returned to the same nest site (if they had not been unduly disturbed). This has since proved to be a regular pattern of all storm petrel marriages studied. So long as both shall live they are faithful to the same nest site, and so to each other.

It is a nice general rule in birds that if the sexes are virtually identical in appearance, colour and size, they are monogamous. The large majority of sea birds fit this description; in addition, in such birds the mated pair invariably share the duties of incubation and feeding the family equally. Sea birds which nest in the open are often handsomely coloured or marked; it is hard for the observer to tell which is male and which female except when coition takes place, or when the female is seen to lay an egg. (Occasionally coition is attempted in reverse by an ardent female mounting the male; although this is unusual and probably unsuccessful.) But bright plumage colour and pattern do have the purpose of mutual advertisement, of visual attention to each other during daylight, bringing the pair close together both for courtship at the start of the breeding season, and later when one partner returns to the nest from foraging or other daily activity.

We have seen that voice is important in signalling to each other, and whips up mutual excitement as the returning bird appears within hearing or

Oystercatchers with their downy young

sight. In a colony of many pairs there is a cacophony of calling confusing to the human ear; and it is not surprising that as the mate of the bird at the nest alights within touching distance, each displays a mixture of threat and appeasement. This behaviour is an automatic temporary reassertion of the fear or defensive reaction by which the individual has learned by experience to protect itself from attack by other birds; but mate recognition quickly follows this first reaction, the aggressive calls change to quieter complacent noises, and there is a bowing or turning away of the conspicuous face pattern and eyes in submissive gestures, as the pair meet and stand or sit at the nest together.

Mutual preening often follows, each nibbling gently the plumage (especially the neck) of the other; not so much a function of hygiene and cleaning away parasites—from which the habit has probably developed—as a sublimated activity and substitute for copulation, helping to maintain the emotional bond which will keep the pair interested in each other during the subsequent long period and duties of incubation and rearing. These actions or love-ceremonies are easily observed in those birds which conduct them in the open by day; their different patterns are fascinating to watch in the three species of gulls, three species of auks, and the oystercatchers which nested in number at Skokholm. The gulls, razorbills and guillemots displayed at the nest, which each mated pair jealously guarded from alien intrusion; but the puffins and oystercatchers, with their red legs and conspicuous bills, moved about within a radius of several metres of the nest

Herring gulls displaying

site, exchanging remarks and gestures with neighbours, the oystercatchers trilling noisily, the puffins almost silent but relieving tension by a comical 'nose-rubbing' of the huge painted bill, a touching, shaking and shoving contest. In the dense puffin assemblies fighting would be a disruptive business, and although a few fights do occur, honour is normally satisfied by harmless display. Such display, whether mutual between partners or directed against strangers, is functional: it 'lets off steam', and is a displacement activity and substitute for the normal performance of a different intention. Thus puffins, gulls and many nest-making birds, finding their mate obstinately remaining on the nest when they wish to incubate, will pick up a stick or stone, and carry it about to relieve frustration (as a man will clench a fist or kick a chair). Instead of wasteful fighting, male gulls will tear at the ground—as they face each other in competition for mate or territory—in redirected attack.

The Mated Pair's Routine

But what happens by night in our storm-petrel colony? It is hard to observe natural display between the mated couple, but from the little we have glimpsed under brief torchlight inspection (and other observers have recorded) at the nest, there is mutual preening as the pair meet in the darkness and sit side-by-side or face each other. Although the birds cannot see each other, such mutual preening and fondling is excitatory and, before the egg is laid, stimulates copulation. No one, to my knowledge, has published any record of coition witnessed in storm petrels, but it seems almost certain that it takes place in the privacy of the nesting crevice, the only site where these ocean wanderers are in close body contact for several hours.

Gradually a clearer picture of the routine of the mated pair emerged from the study of the successful, as well as the failed, nests. It was disappointing to find that the egg in some crevices might be left cold for one or more days—due entirely, as I at first believed, to my spying visits and occasional hooking forth of the brooding adult to check its band-number. Later I and other observers were to discover that in some of these nests the egg had been left cold temporarily, even permanently, from natural causes.

Banded adults were the first to return to marked nests in the spring, during the first two weeks of May. Many more, all unbanded, appeared to swell the population later in May, throughout June and well into July. The majority of these late arrivals were non-breeders, as described later. For approximately $6\frac{1}{2}$ weeks before the egg is laid, the mated pair pay visits somewhat erratically by night to the site, sometimes together, sometimes singly. But occupation by day during that period is comparatively rare. In 28 burrows studied by Peter Davis in these same hedge-walls, he recorded 439 night visits, but only 117 occasions when petrels remained by day, before the egg was laid.

Subsequent studies have established that in storm petrels, as in the shearwaters I had under observation, and in most tubenosed birds, it is the male which arrives first in the breeding period. Clearly it is important that he be ready to mate at any time that the female is. His function essentially is to locate the site, adopt it and maintain possession by advertising his presence with the purring call, which will attract a mate to join him. The mature male is naturally by experience strongly attached to the burrow where he achieved a successful partnership the previous year. And so is the female, if she is his partner of yesteryear. The pair meet again, but although he is ready and capable of a fertile mating, she is at first most likely not. She needs the stimulation of courtship, of preening and fondling before she is able to ovulate. One can imagine, from watching the behaviour at the nest of related diurnal tubenosed species such as the albatrosses and fulmars, that when the female storm petrel is quite ready to mate, the fond nibbling and preening in the darkness enables the male to obtain a firm grip on the head or nape feathers of the female with his bill, and this contact stimulates her to crouch low, her wings open slightly to form a platform for the male to mount, long enough to twist his tail around and below hers, which she erects as soon as she feels his weight on her back. Sperm is transferred by a gland, rather than a true penis, when the male cloaca is inserted into the female cloaca by the pressure of momentary violent joining.

How often and how long before the egg is laid mating takes place is not known. The domestic hen can lay fertile eggs up to twenty, and the turkey to thirty, days after copulation. What is known is that the female storm petrel usually leaves the nest as soon as the egg is laid, when the male takes it over and incubates it for as long as his mate is absent. In the larger tubenoses— albatross, fulmar and shearwater—this period when the female is immediately off-duty after laying her egg may last several days while the male incubates (royal and wandering albatrosses, two to three weeks; the short-tailed shearwater *Puffinus tenuirostris*, studied by my friend Dom Serventy in the Bass Strait, twelve to fourteen days; prions and storm petrels rarely more than two to three days). In case the male is not present on the night or day when the egg is laid, his partner usually remains for one or two days until he reappears. But not infrequently the female, no doubt hungry and impatient to go to sea, does not wait so long; in which case the egg is left cold for that period. At this stage, before the embryo has started to develop, chilling does not matter so much: there are records of eggs left cold early in the incubation period for up to eleven days which, nevertheless, successfully hatched.

Serventy's model study of the Tasmanian muttonbird (as the short-tailed

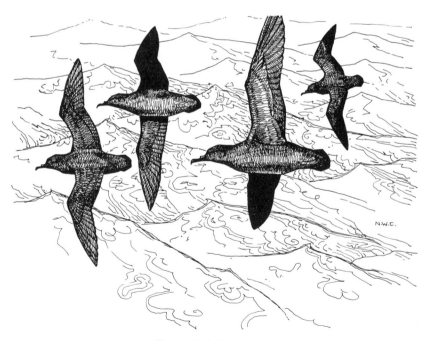

Short-tailed shearwaters

shearwater *Puffinus tenuirostris* is called in Australia) has indicated a pattern of pre-egg behaviour by male and female which seems to hold good for most of the tubenoses, including the storm petrels. In general the mature males arrive first to spring-clean and take possession of the burrow. Their calling soon attracts a partner from the adult females which fly home a few nights later. One or both of the pair occasionally remain by day in this early period, but most of these established breeders return before dawn to feed at sea. The peak of spermatogenesis is reached about a month after the first appearance of the male, which means that fertile mating is at its height then, after the home burrow has been much visited by both. What little furnishing occurs has been completed—a little desultory, almost accidental, scraping together of loose material picked up in the burrow entrance, and deposited in the slight scrape in the earth, which will contain the single egg.

The meagre dark home under the ground or in the rocks, is ready for the egg. Now occurs an exodus which may seem strange, but is really advantageous, especially for the female. The entire population (of the muttonbird colony) vacates the nesting burrows for about three weeks, until egg-laying begins—quite punctually—on the three nights of 19–21 November (in the southern spring). There is remarkable synchronisation of each important event in the annual cycle of this tubenose, which breeds in vast numbers on the Bass Strait Islands; a synchronisation which must have evolved through competition for nesting burrows under pressure of such numbers. The pre-egg exodus is clearly important for the female to build up her condition by a period of heavy feeding at sea to nourish and produce her large egg; while the male, who has fasted for the longer period spent ashore in preparing and guarding the burrow, and in subsequent mating, also has need to recuperate by feeding. As we have seen he will take over the egg as soon as it is laid, and will have to fast yet again until he is relieved by his mate returning from sea. Other shearwaters, including the sooty *Puffinus griseus* and the Manx *P. puffinus*, achieve a similar but not quite so precise synchronisation. But not the storm petrel: egg-laying is spread over a much longer period, for various reasons which are not very clear, but probably associated with seasonal food-supply. (In our studies of marked birds their tendency to desert when handled produced a further unevenness in incubation and fledging periods, which undoubtedly delayed these un-naturally.)

Egg-laying in our storm petrel reaches a peak during the third week in June, and after dropping slightly during the next ten days it rises even higher between 30 June and 5 July, then ceases abruptly. The second peak is associated with the late arrival of inexperienced females, laying their first-ever egg later than the mature females. Thus at this time, with the summer solstice already past, activity at the petrel colony is at its most intense.

The Egg

The majority of birds which nest in deep holes or burrows lay white or near-white eggs—a colour which is more easily seen in semi-darkness. The egg of all the storm petrels is no exception. It looks, and often is, perfectly white when new laid; but when held up to the light, exhibits a varying zone or ring of reddish brown spots concentrated around the blunt end of this typically symmetrical ovate egg. This fades as incubation proceeds. Average measurements of British storm-petrel eggs are 28 × 21mm, with a range of 25–30 × 19–23mm.

In case the egg is lost within a day or so of laying, a replacement may be produced, although rarely. Once incubation is well advanced physiological changes in the female metabolism (as in broody hens) prevent further ovulation. Younger, later-arriving, females do not lay a second egg to replace the not infrequent loss of their first, a loss due largely to inexperience.

Sharing incubation

Some individual petrels nesting deep in stone screes or at the end of long winding earthen burrows may never see their mate, egg or chick. They depend on voice recognition and individual scent when the incoming bird, calling and shuffling towards the nest, reaches its partner. What discussions go on then! If you have the imagination I am blessed or cursed with, you may try to put their talk into words: 'So there you are! What a relief—my dear! I've waited long enough, three days and nights alone—nice to have a good long sleep at first, but really, you seemed to be so long at sea, I wondered if you had got lost or killed . . .'

'Not a bit. After that last spell on guard at the nest, while you were away having a good time among the sardines and shrimps, I wondered the same thing—that you must be lost forever and I would have to incubate our wonderful egg all alone for as long as it takes! I was getting hungry, and was just about to go off to feed myself when you turned up . . .'

This is the pattern revealed in our, and other, storm-petrel studies: each partner two or three days away at sea fattening up for the shift of two or three days on the egg. But do they talk so intelligently, lovingly to each other, in the utter darkness? I have no proof that they do. Yet this swift ocean traveller, living so hardily at sea for most of its life, with its sepia-dark shining eye that copes both with darkness over the land and direct and brilliant reflected sunlight at sea, seems with that eye to flash a message of some sort, perhaps of incomprehending wonder, perhaps a plea to you, as you hold one in your hand, as if it were saying:

'You will never understand fully our marvellous way of life, our freedom to wander the ocean, our ability to outlast great storms, to find our way each summer to this tiny crevice on a remote island. Is it not enough that we do this without harming your interests? In this, our special sea and aerial way of life, we are far more efficient and intelligent than you clumsy land animals, clad in unnatural garments robbed from other creatures. Not that we are interested in you, except to desire you leave us in peace and give up this meddling in our personal lives . . .'

'Forgive me, I only desire to know the answer to so many questions about your mysterious life. For one thing, since at home you only meet your mate by night in near or total darkness, do you ever meet, see, or know him or her in daylight at sea?'

'Of course not—not deliberately. That's not important. At sea we are busy feeding, or migrating, or moulting. Should we meet accidentally at sea, we should recognise each other by voice, but . . .'

'But what about scent, I mean individual odour?'

'You ask silly questions. We are not interested in each other except to make love at home, privately in the dark; and to rear our child. At other times, away at sea, we have to keep feeding, to weather the occasional great storm and stay alive. No personal ties then. Enjoy life as we travel to the sun and escape the winter. Feed when food is plentiful, put on fat for the bad times, and sleep now and then when we find ourselves in a rare calm. But we prefer rough weather—so much easier to fly when the wind has a good lift in it . . .'

Weighing the incubating storm petrel has proved that the incoming bird never feeds the stay-at-home, in those nests where brief night visits by the bird off-duty have been recorded. The plump incoming partner needs the stored food and fat gained in feeding at sea to tide it over the subsequent fasting period while incubating. Davis records a three-day shift at the nest in which a male lost weight from 33.5 to 29 grams.

Although I and other observers have recorded visits by night of unattached birds, rarely remaining by day in a burrow owned by a long-established marked pair, these visits, as already mentioned, cease as soon as incubation begins. It is difficult to find out what is going on when a third bird enters a burrow in this way, since attempts to study them by artificial light instantly inhibit natural behaviour. During the few quick flashes of my torch upon a stranger in the same burrow with one of the established pair I could see no evidence of fighting. The visit seemed peaceful and tolerated. As to the reason for visiting, presumably the stranger is seeking a mate?

The incubation period

My first six incubation periods ranged from 38 to 40 days, average 39.5 days. Thirty-six incubation periods recorded by Davis averaged slightly more—40.6 days; but in some ten of these the egg was left cold for between one and eleven days (deducted from the total, only days of incubation counted), resulting in chilling which must have retarded development. Undoubtedly this neglect of the egg in these cases was largely due to human interference. Therefore, allowing for such interference temporarily slowing down the development of the embryo, the minimum period of incubation of *Hydrobates pelagicus* is thirty-eight days. In all other storm-petrel species discussed later in this book, it will be shown that, where carefully recorded, the true minimum incubation period is about the same, thirty-eight to forty-one days. The slightly larger white-faced species (page 155) has a slightly longer incubation period; but it catches up, so to speak, by a somewhat shorter fledging period, to reach the average of all storm petrels of around one hundred days from the laying of the egg to the departure of the grown nestling.

In my study of the Manx shearwater I had already found that on some days early in the incubation period (which lasts a minimum of fifty days) the egg might be left cold, usually for one but occasionally more days, without resulting in the death of the embryo. Since that study, over fifty years ago, careful observers of several tubenose species have shown that marked eggs under study may still hatch, although temporarily abandoned during incubation, but usually early in the period and most often for one or two days immediately after laying, before the embryo has started intensive development, warmed by the parental body-heat. Many birds, such as game birds, which lay larger clutches of up to twelve eggs, do not begin incubation until the last egg is laid, thereby synchronising hatching. But careful observation of incubation by single-egg shearwaters and storm petrels, under minimum human disturbance, has shown that 'neglect' of the egg probably occurs naturally as well, and sometimes for long periods, later during the incubation.

The phenomenon has attracted increasing interest and is discussed by Boersma & Wheelwright (1979). They studied the fork-tailed storm petrel *Oceanodroma furcata* on the Barren Islands, Alaska (see page 128). Of thirty-three nests in which the chicks hatched, the mean number of days of egg neglect during incubation was high—eleven days during which the egg remained cold, in burrows where the average temperature was 10 °C. (They tried to minimise human handling and disturbance leading to desertion of the egg by a now standard procedure I have already described: placing a gate of small sticks upright across the entrance of the nest burrow to record visits.)

Probably the main cause of these 'natural' gaps in incubation is the failure of the off-duty bird to return before the sitting bird departs; in other known instances one of the pair has disappeared altogether, probably lost at sea, leaving the bereaved partner to incubate as it may—between intervals of days away to recuperate. But whatever the cause, there is a remarkably high tolerance by the petrel embryo to chilling over many days. Boersma & Wheelwright conclude that this tolerance is 'adaptive in an environment where storms are severe and unpredictable and food resources are patchy. Distant foraging and long incubation periods, characteristic of these birds, increase the probability that storms and undependable food resources will delay an individual's returning to relieve its incubating partner'.

The maximum single period of egg-neglect in this Alaskan storm petrel was seven days; compare this with the single period of eleven days recorded by Davis for our storm petrel. Long periods for such a small embryo to survive chilling; but as we shall see, when the embryo does hatch, it is capable of surviving similar periods of several days and nights of neglect. But if the egg is neglected for any reason longer than perhaps a week to ten days consecutively, the embryo does not usually survive. In that case one, or each in turn, of the parents may return to continue incubating the egg past the normal incubation period, until it becomes rotten and breaks, or they abandon it. I have found cold storm-petrel eggs with dead embryos, and less often eggs which seemed to be infertile—with no sign of development—in burrows from which the adults had long departed, at the end of the breeding season. Davis records a similar experience.

Body temperature
Birds generally have a slightly higher average body temperature than man's, which is 37°C. Disparate sizes of birds, from ostriches to tits and storm petrels, have around the same body temperature of 40°C. Roberts (1940) gives the average body temperature of ten adult Wilson's storm petrels breeding in Graham Land, Antarctica, as 38.8°C (range 40.5° max, 36.5° min), the outside temperature being close to freezing. Beck & Brown (1972) by means of a thermistor probe determined the average temperature within a Wilson's-petrel egg being naturally incubated in a marked nest in the South Orkneys over an unspecified number of days, as 36°C. Despite the near-freezing summer climate of these places, the incubating bird is able to maintain the temperature of the egg close to that of the bare brood patch which is well supplied with numerous subcutaneous veins or arteries circulating warm blood for the purpose. At Skokholm D. A. Scott (1970) found the 'incubation temperature' of *Hydrobates pelagicus* did not exceed 32°C, a figure it is hard to understand, unless it represents the temperature of the *outside* of the egg warmed under the parental brood patch.

Hatching, from the moment when the beak of the chick first punctures the shell to its complete emergence, takes seldom less than forty-eight hours, during which, and until the chick has dried out, the egg remains tucked into the warm brood patch. One parent remains to keep the chick warm for the first week, for a good reason. Although the new-hatched chick has a plentiful, usually thick, down, with bare patches about the face (and in some storm-petrel babies, including *Hydrobates*, a bald crown), to help keep it warm, its body temperature will fall to that of the air temperature if it is parted from the parental source of heat. This of course is fatal in those species hatched in low or nearly zero air temperatures.

With feeding, however, the chick quickly puts on a layer of fat and acquires the homoiothermic state of the parent. Roberts (1940) measured the body temperature of 13 Wilson's-petrel chicks of known age, and records the Celsius temperature of two one-day-olds at 25° and 27°; of two two-day-olds at 28° and 30°; one four-day-old at 32.8°; one seven-day-old at 36.5°.

After one week the parents no longer remain in the nest with the chick. It has reached close to normal adult temperature, enabling it to survive without further parental brooding, provided it is well fed. Also its down has grown longer, and therefore warmer.

4

The nestling

Our new-born British storm petrel is a limp feeble morsel of life normally weighing only 5–6g when dry after twelve to twenty-four hours. Its eyes are closed, as if the lids were glued together; but sight is of no immediate use to it in the darkness of the burrow, under the parental breast. It has made its presence known acoustically long before, as soon as it broke through the inner membrane with the sharp egg-tooth near the tip of its upper mandible, and breathed air in the closed sac at the wide end of the egg.

Hatching the chick is the supreme moment of achievement in the annual cycle of the parents, and they behave accordingly, as if as proud of the child as human parents are of their new-born. The difference is that the storm petrel mother or father cannot see the baby in the darkness. It is merely a querulous tapping at first, then a cheeping voice, and at last a wet, somewhat slimy presence as it bursts forth. But the voice, calling for help sometimes even before the shell is broken, a muffled peeping, is eagerly heard (and almost certainly answered) by the loving and now anxious adult on incubation duty. This could be mother or father, by day; but except by night, rarely both. Thus the bond of voice-recognition and body-touching is soon established between child and parents. The object of intense parental care has changed from a smooth neat enclosed capsule of developing embryo to a disorderly sprawling downy object needing warmth at first, and calling for nourishment later, once the egg-yolk attached to the large infant stomach is absorbed within.

British storm petrel and chick in burrow

There is often a seemingly tedious delay lasting up to seventy-two hours, but usually under thirty hours, before complete emergence. One observer has reported that the parent on duty may sometimes help the cramped and confined chick to escape from the shell by nibbling tenderly around the initial opening it has made. But this intimacy must be very difficult to observe, and I have not seen it myself in our storm petrel. Normally the unhatched chick, which as an embryo is slung hammock-style by the rope-like chalaza, was frequently moved about when the egg was turned at intervals by the incubating bird. Now it turns around at hatching time in a complete circle, as it instinctively hammers at the outer membrane and shell beyond the air sac, until the cap is severed and pushed aside by the next movements. The large legs, folded forward under the stomach in the embryo, are pressed downward, the back of the head is pushed up against the loosened cap, and suddenly the head falls out, or rears up, the long neck being stretched for the first time.

In most birds at hatching time this violent exercise temporarily exhausts the youngster, and it may lie some time with its rear still resting half within the shell. Usually in this position is excretes for the last time before complete emergence, leaving this faecal matter behind in the shell, with other nitrogenous waste voided and accumulated during incubation and normally contained in a gelatinous sac; nature provides that the ammonia in this waste reacts with other substances to produce uric acid, almost insoluble and relatively harmless to the unborn bird. Apart from the faecal sac, the shell is clean and sanitary within. In some species the empty shell is carried away from the nest (most passerines), or eaten (kiwi), thus removing evidence which might attract the attention of predators or unwelcome scavengers. The storm petrel ignores the discarded shell entirely; it is pushed to one side, or sometimes trampled flat. I have found it lying at the back of the burrow, where it may remain for the winter before gradually disintegrating. (On Skokholm I suspect that the mouse would be hungry enough during winter to devour an empty egg-shell.) The shell is porous, allowing gas to escape during incubation; it is composed of about 95 per cent calcium carbonate, and would be edible and nourishing to a lime-deficient animal (I have watched vegetarian sheep eat the calcium-rich legs and beaks of dead birds killed at a lighthouse in the Orkney Islands).

The emerged chick enjoys a period of relaxation, of stretching its liberated legs and neck, and the stumps of tiny wings, while absorbing the egg-yolk, warmly hidden in contact with the naked skin of the parental brood patch. There in the darkness or twilight of its larger prison below ground the infant petrel sleeps or rests during its first few days and nights of late July or early August. Above ground the island's summer flowers, conditioned by the strong ocean wind and pressure of grazing rabbits, make

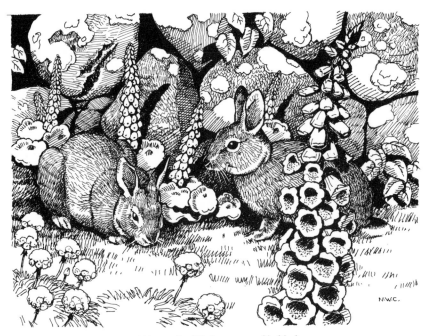

Rabbits and wild flowers on Skokholm

their usual bright display at this season: white stars of eyebright and pearlwort, rosy sandwort spurrey, yellow of tormentil, pink English stonecrop, and abundant wild thyme, its sweet scent on a sunlit day mingling with the musky air emanating from the petrel burrows. On the shady side of the hedge-walls the short spikes of navelwort exhibit their green-yellow tubular flowers with those of woodsage. From the foot of the wall the pink-purple bells of the foxglove are rifled of nectar by the large bumble-bees of Skokholm. But the colours of wild flowers, so pleasing to the human eye, mean nothing to our storm petrels, seeing them only as dark shapes as they fly home by night. Probably (but how prove it?) all species of storm petrels, themselves robed in black and white, and other sea birds which attend their nests only at night, are colour-blind, seeing only in tones of white, grey and black.

Care of the Chick

The eyelids of the chick become unstuck and open about the fifth day. During this blind period the chick normally rests with its bill touching the ground, as if the head were too heavy to be held upright—as seen when the parental breast is lifted by our enquiring wire probe. At this stage, and for a few days earlier during the last days of incubation, the parent on duty was bolder in defying our wire, and would peck at it defensively, such was its anxiety to protect its treasure. In the early days of incubation, and later during the fledging period, it shuffled away from the advancing wire to the back of the nest cavity.

The first food is supplied to the semi-helpless youngster as soon as it is lively enough to indicate hunger. This it does by the peeping call and by thrusting its beak up towards the parental throat—in the manner typical of other sea birds, but especially of the tubenose family. This up-thrusting, combined with a rapid vibration of the chick's bill and throat, stimulates the adult to open its own bill, and bend down to touch and manoeuvre the infant bill so that it presses crosswise (at right angles) within the jaws of the parent. In this position the adult tongue touches the vibrating tongue of the chick; and the parent proceeds to pump food from its stomach into its throat, but in a controlled manner. The adult throat appears to contract enough for the flow of food to be regulated to the amount the nestling is able to swallow comfortably. During the actual passage of the transferred food, which is semi-liquid, the windpipe entrance to the lungs of both birds, immediately behind the tongue, must automatically close to avoid choking.

In this controlled fashion the chick receives in small doses just as much nourishment as it can immediately hold in throat and crop. After each regurgitation, lasting perhaps only a few seconds, the temporarily sated chick withdraws its bill, and both gulp down what food is left in their throats. There is a pause of several seconds, even minutes, before the chick, if still hungry, lifts its head again and pleads for more. Nature has provided that in the tubenoses the first and early feeds are small in quantity and predigested to a soup-like or thick-oil consistency suited to the tender digestion of the infant stomach. Small, but also frequent, depending on the growing appetite of the child and what is still available in the parental crop. So long as both last the chick may be fed at intervals during the day, as well as at night.

At this time of considerable excitement over the hatching period, the bird away foraging at sea usually returns each night with a crop full of food, eager to take over the brooding and feeding duties. One could well imagine a domestic dispute arising . . .

'Great seas and gales! I wasn't expecting you until I've got rid of this cropload of fish soup. Little Hydrobates hasn't taken half the supply I've been keeping warm in my stomach. He's too young yet. You'd better go back to sea and feed yourself up for another twenty-four hours.'

'Nonsense, I'm bursting with shrimp and little fishes. You must have lost a lot of weight feeding little Hydro for a whole day since I last came home. Off you go, and you needn't come back for at least two nights, while baby and I are digesting the load I've brought home . . .'

This excitement and anxiety of both parents (which will wane shortly) is a natural insurance or safeguard that the young bird in its first helpless week, by this nightly exchange of the guard, will be adequately warmed and fed, with reserves of food available all day. Such a reserve is vitally necessary when occasionally, by some accident of weather, or the death of one parent, the bird on duty is not relieved by its partner. The brooding adult will not willingly leave the child alone for the first week. During that time, and longer if the bird off-duty has been away for days before the egg hatched, the lone brooding bird will have exhausted the stored food in its stomach, and presently will have nothing substantial to give the child getting hungrier and demanding to be fed.

In this emergency it is probable, although difficult to prove except by continuous watch at the nest which so far has not been possible, that if the hungry chick persists in reaching at the parental beak for food, the reaction of the adult will be to go through the motions of feeding. If so, it will almost certainly bring up a small quantity of the residual secretions of the proventriculus, if there is no semi-digested sea-food left in the stomach. It is even probable that the chick's persistent nibbling of the adult beak will eventually stimulate (as excitement can stimulate bile flow in man) that oily secretion (which is also a food) of the stomach walls to flow afresh. We have already referred to the ability of the emperor penguin to feed its new-born chick from a stomach which has been denied food for more than three months. And, whenever I have handled a brooding storm petrel which has been several days alone at the nest, it has ejected the typical musky oil. Of course, if straight from the sea during the rearing period, the adult storm petrel will throw up more solid food—identifiable parts of small squid, fish and zooplankton.

It is with this material that the nestling is nourished. At first it is doled out in a well-digested state as a reddish oil, but as the chick rapidly grows it is able to swallow a thicker soup. As already remarked, storm petrels cease to brood their chick by day after the first week, although occasionally one parent may be present by day up to the twelfth day. But during the second week of the chick's life both parents usually come home with food each night. From the fifth day onwards the chick has become homoiothermic (able to maintain normal body heat without brooding by the adult), its body further protected from low temperatures by the rapidly growing down. Thus, stoked with fuel, it is able both to grow and to maintain that steady temperature.

The Chick's Plumage

The young storm petrel is not as large as a ping-pong ball when dry after hatching. The blue-grey, almost silvery-grey, natal down however is comparatively long on the upper parts—average 6mm. The bald patch on the crown of the head is pinkish at birth, but quickly darkens and becomes covered with new down by the tenth day. The face remains bare until the first feathers start growing about the fifth week. The bill and legs lack pigment at first, but the bill is large and becomes black about the twentieth day, and the legs are dark about the thirtieth. The little white egg-tooth at the bend of the upper mandible falls off within the first week.

The long 'double' down characteristic of some nestling tubenoses has an oiliness which must help keep warmth in and repel moisture, especially in those species (albatross, cape pigeon) nesting in the open in high cold latitudes. In the storm petrel the second (mesoptile) down begins to sprout from the same follicle as the first down (protoptile). This second down grows as long as the first, which remains attached to the tip of the new growth. At the end of the third week the chick resembles a powder-puff of velvety grey-blue down, when held quietly in the palm of the hand. Only the large black hooked beak is visible as the head, with beady black eye and pale new down on the face, is withdrawn into the fluffy ball. If the wing is examined at this age in a well-fed chick, the tips of the primaries are just visible emerging from their sheaths; tail-quills or rectrices sprout within another week.

As the feathers of the body develop rapidly after the thirtieth day, they push out the down from the same follicle, so that each feather has a plume of down at its tip, even the young wing and tail quills. This double down gradually breaks away as the young bird becomes more lively in the nest. By the time the chick is completely feathered at fifty days, the down is abraded from the head, as a result of feeding contact with the parents, and during its own preening movements. It still forms a mat or cushion on the lower part of the breast, and some tufts linger upon the wings and back. Little or no down is visible externally by the sixtieth day, in a normal healthy chick. Undernourished chicks take longer to moult the down and acquire their first full plumage. This is almost identical in colour and markings to the mature plumage of the adults, except that in the old breeding birds, with the annual moult approaching if not already begun, the plumage is faded, the black now almost rusty brown, and the whitish tips of some feathers quite worn away. The two-months-old nestling (now a fledgeling) wears a brighter coat, all black save for the conspicuous white rump; the face, including forehead and chin around the deep black bill, is greyer. In fresh plumage both adult and juvenile have narrow white edges to upper and under wing-coverts, which appear as a slight white bar in flight, seen close to. The slightly rounder tail is quite distinct from the forked tail of Leach's storm petrel inhabiting the same Atlantic coast—a good identification mark at sea. In the hand the tip of the outer flight (primary) feather is pointed in the juvenile before moult; in the adult this wing feather is rounded.

Feeding and Growth

The natural food of the tiny storm petrels—smallest of all sea birds—is low down in the oceanic food chain, but no lower than that of the largest animals the world has ever known—the baleen whales. They subsist on the same organisms of the zooplankton: adult and immature forms of molluscs and crustaceans, especially the euphausid shrimps, and small or immature fish and squid. The zooplankton feeds on the lowest, minute life in the chain, the phytoplankton: microscopic plant life, diatoms and algae floating free at or near the surface. These are most abundant in cold and temperate seas where turbulence and upwelling are caused by strong winds and currents, which bring to the surface constantly the essential salts and minerals—phosphate, nitrogen, potash and calcium—derived from dissolved rocks and dead and decayed organisms. These are used by the phytoplankton, which photo-synthesises, grows and multiplies. In warm regions of tropical calm near the equator where there is little movement of the ocean, these nourishing minerals and dead organisms sink to the cold bottom of the still, often deep, water, which is almost de-oxygenated. Except where strong tides and seasonal monsoons disturb shallower water near islands and coasts, there is little food available to attract storm petrels and other surface zooplankton feeders. Baleen whales, which find tropical seas desirably warm for the birth of their young, are believed to fast here during their parturition and mating sojourn in these tropical or semi-tropical latitudes, being fat from previous feeding in higher latitudes. As we shall describe later in this book the storm petrels which make long-distance migrations across the equator are evidently well equipped with fat reserves for their journey through less fertile seas.

Once the young petrel is hatched and able to maintain its own body heat after the first week, both parents are able to devote the hours of daylight to collecting food, eating enough to nourish themselves, and by night bringing home the surplus to feed their child. From an initial birthweight when dry of 5–6g, the chick's weight increases in proportion to the number of feeds it is given each night by one or both parents. Peter Davis records that this increase, ascertained by weighing the chick immediately after it had been fed at night, varied around 2g in each of the first ten nights, and up to 23g per night subsequently. Naturally the biggest gains were made when both parents returned to the nest in the same night. He found that after an average overnight gain of 12g the nestling had retained, by its weight recorded before nightfall the following day, two-thirds (8g), and lost the other third by natural respiration and defecation. Average size by weight of night feeds increased from 5g in the first week to 6.7g in the fourth week, then levelled off to a maximum weight of 6.8g in the seventh week. Early in its life the food taken by the chick sometimes doubled its weight overnight.

Frequency of night visits to feed the nestling declines during the seventh week. In the last five nights before the young storm petrel left Skokholm, the average feed per night was down to 4.5g. Davis found that 'feeds of average size weighed from 30–40 per cent of the nestling's body weight just after the end of brooding, and only about 10 per cent near fledging-time'. It is unusual to find an adult remaining at the nest by day after the first week, but it does occur rarely up to the sixteenth day (Davis), and once I found a parent with a chick which was thirty-three days old—perhaps it had overslept after feeding the child, and dawn had surprised it? On all these occasions the parent is seen to be resting *beside*, not attempting to brood, the large downy chick. On the thirty-third day the nestling appeared as bulky as the adult, from the extent of its double down.

During the sixty-one or sixty-two days the youngster remains in the nest from hatching to fledging, it consumes on average about 310g (just over 11oz). It reaches its greatest weight of 42g about the fiftieth day, and is then much heavier than the adult, which has an average weight of 28g. The normal fledgeling, fed on most nights by one or both parents during the first fifty days, then perhaps less regularly during the last ten days or so, is, I found, in fat condition and ready to fly away to sea at any time between the fifty-fourth and sixty-fourth day of its life.

But there are some chicks which are not so fortunate, either from having lost one parent, or from an inadequate supply of food. If this occurs late in the first fifty days it is not so serious; by then the chick has acquired a good covering of fat and can survive a short fast. But if the chick, as sometimes happens, is neglected earlier, over several days, its growth is retarded and it takes proportionately longer to fledge; and in cases of longer neglect it must die of starvation. In the breeding seasons 1966–9 at Skokholm, Scott (1970) records a mean nestling period of sixty-eight days: these summers seem to have been bad weather ones, delaying fledging.

A storm-petrel chick left unbrooded at Skokholm during the first two or three days after hatching will usually die of chill if the weather is cold, but later it develops a remarkable resistance to both cold and lack of food during any abnormal absence of its parents. Such long-neglected chicks are able to survive without food by a general cooling down of body temperature and reduction of heartbeat. It is almost as if the chick was beginning to hibernate; in your hand such a neglected young bird feels cold, as if dying, and is too sluggish to vomit as a well-fed chick does. The same survival device, a slowing-down of the rate of metabolism, occurs in some other species of birds where gaps of several days may occur between feeds brought to the young; notably in the young common swift *Apus apus*, when the parents are prevented by cold weather from collecting an adequate supply of insect food. The tiny species of humming birds, which need to eat almost their own weight in food daily, would starve at night if they did not reduce their rate of heartbeat and temperature, and become—to the human hand, when I have tried lifting them from their perch at night—quite cold and rigid in night-hibernation. They need to be warmed artificially before they will revive, open their eyes and take flight.

We have already described (page 44) the ability of the embryo storm petrel within the egg to survive for up to eleven days when the egg is left cold continuously during that period. In the same way as the neglected egg can be warmed into life and development again, the long-neglected and hungry chick can be warmed by a parent and fed back to life and development. But there are time limits, and a price to pay: incubation and fledging periods are extended in relation to the length of the period of neglect. And such long neglect results in a less vigorous, physically smaller fledgeling leaving the nest, weighing less than normal.

Thus one chick in one of my marked nests in 1931 was sixty-eight days before it flew to sea. Hatched on 14 August, it was well fed during the first three weeks (although I did not visit it every night then, for fear of causing parental desertion). But with my matchstick 'gates' to prove the occasions of parental visits at night, I found this chick was visited (and presumed fed) on only six nights between 5 and 15 September. During the first twenty-one days of October it was visited on not more than seven nights, the last occasion being 15 October. During the last six nights before it took off for the sea, on 21 October, the matchstick guard was unbroken. At that time I was not weighing any of my marked petrels, afraid the disturbance would scare off the parents.

Peter Davis records an even longer fledging period in one of his marked nestlings:

Minor intervals between feeds no doubt cause the chick some discomfort, but do not retard its growth, whilst the longer gaps of the last ten days or so occur when development is virtually complete. The unusual intervals of six nights between feeds at Burrow 20 from the 46th to 52nd days of the chick's life, had interesting consequences. This chick had already been rather poorly fed . . . now its weight declined from 40 to 27 grams in seven days. By the fourth evening it appeared very weak, and on the sixth seemed to be moribund, with eyes closed and little sign of movement. The following morning the chick had been fed, and was remarkably lively. This chick remained some ten days behind normal chicks in plumage development, and particularly in loss of nestling down, although the growth of the primary feathers was not much retarded. It eventually departed (on 20 October 1956) at a rather low weight after a record fledging period of 73 days, but survived to be captured by a fishing vessel off Belle Ile, W. France, in late December 1956.

Increasing gaps between parental visits towards the end of the fledging period are attributed by Davis to 'increasing loss of interest in the chick, though in general it is not possible to speak of a desertion period in this petrel'. But only in four of his thirty-two nests under observation in three summers was the chick fed on the same night as it departed. In his other nests the chick was deserted—as I believe is more normal: it remained unvisited for up to seven nights before it departed. But we should note that the full-grown chick is restless at this stage, around the sixtieth day, and human handling and weighing may well cause it to fly to sea a few days earlier than it would naturally. Scott (1970) considers that 'few chicks are deserted by their parents more than three or four days before departure'.

Hygiene

Although the nestling consumes on average some 310g of food intake during its development of approximately two months before it leaves the nest, and the waste is daily voided in the burrow, the storm-petrel's home is never insanitary. The whitish faecal matter is semi-liquid and ejected with enough force to be spread around the walls, generally away from the entrance of the nesting place, in the form of a thin coat of 'whitewash'. This dries rapidly, or is absorbed by the dry earth if the site is a burrow in the ground. The chick remains clean, from the time it dries out from the egg to the moment of departure. With its large bill it preens and oils its body, down and feathers as soon as it has full control of its head movements after the first week of comparative helplessness described above.

Preening, washing and body care in birds is a reaction to itchiness caused by irritation of the nerves just below the skin, as in human beings; an irritation due partly to internal causes (natural movement of blood, and occasionally endoparasites living below the skin), and partly to feather disarrangement, and to external parasites. The last are generally specific to the species, or to the family to which the bird belongs, and consist of feather mites and feather lice living permanently on or inside the feathers on which they feed, also of non-specific adult fleas and ticks which are temporary visitors—blood-suckers which, although summer parasites of the storm petrel, spend the winter in larval form in or near the nest (see Appendix, page 183). The common grey-black tick, genus *Ixodes*, which is often plentiful on islands where sea birds are numerous (it has not infrequently attached itself to me during bird-banding operations at Skokholm!), frequently attacks the puffin in such numbers that its white face is discoloured by these clinging, sucking brutes; it also settles upon the brooding albatross of southern islands. But I have found it only twice on a nestling storm petrel—fortunately for the petrel. On so small a bird this large tick, which usually attaches to the barer parts, chiefly the head and feet, of its victims, must be a serious drain on the blood supply, as well as a great irritation. It attaches to its host stealthily (it is said painlessly, by injecting saliva containing an anaesthetic), and buries its beak, anchored with recurved spines, into the flesh too firmly for the host to preen it off. However, when fully engorged after about one week, it drops off, and hides below ground to moult into a new larger skin. If it is not yet fully grown it seeks a victim again. If it has mated as a mature female (after several moults), it lays about 3,000 eggs in the ground debris, then dies. With difficulty I would remove ticks from these sea birds, using tweezers with great care so as not to leave the tick's mouthparts to fester in the wound. It was a relief to know that when a puffin or petrel with any ticks attached goes to sea for more than a week (as at the end of the breeding season), the parasites would be drowned when, engorged, they relinquished their hold!

On the little uninhabited island of Burhou, near Alderney in the Channel Isles, one late July night, examining numerous storm-petrel nests in the boulder beach, I found the ground swarming with the common red mite *Dermanyssus gallinae*. This normally hides in crevices all day, and emerges at night to suck the blood of poultry and cage birds, as well as wild birds and other warm-blooded animals—it will attack horses, cattle and people. It is barely 1mm in length, but multiplies in the warmth of late summer with great rapidity. Many mites had attacked petrels. In the earth burrows, occupied by numerous puffins on Burhou and warmed by the summer sun, the mite was so plentiful that it had quite debilitated the young puffins; at this season they were not yet ready to go to sea, but several hundred had left their holes prematurely, to die in the open, evidently from extreme irritation and loss of blood. Those still alive were feeble, lean and bloodless-looking. Probably this mite had been transferred by chance from a local poultry house on Alderney, on the clothes of a summer day-visitor to Burhou. But it had serious consequences some years later, if we can believe that it was the main cause of the reduction of both puffin and storm petrel to their present low numbers, near extinction, on Burhou. Fortunately this mite needs warmth in which to thrive and multiply, and I never found one on cool suboceanic Skokholm in over thirteen years living there, although we had imported and kept chickens during our first years.

5
First flight

The fragile matchstick-brackenstalk gate which I inserted at the entrance (which is also the exit) of the storm-petrel homes under study, to indicate ingress or egress, had already proved indispensable during my earlier and still continuing shearwater research. The device excused me many nights of tedious watching when I was too weary and sleepy after a long summer day fishing, shepherding and tending the garden. More important it reduced the annoyance to the marked birds of too frequent handling which at first had caused unnatural absence, and even desertion of egg or chick. Use of this simple, easily brushed aside, barrier helped to uncover the truth, quite unsuspected previously but now known to be typical of a large number of tubenoses, of the desertion by the Manx shearwater and storm-petrel parents of their single chick before it is ready to go to sea. The reasons are now apparent: the adults have lost interest in the fledgeling because of seasonal changes in their physical condition. They have laboured long enough to rear their child to independence, but now their plumage is worn, faded, frayed and beginning to moult; normally it will be renewed completely during the southward migration of the autumn and in winter quarters. In both storm petrel and shearwater some of the adult feathers are moulted late during incubation and while the young are being fed; even a few wing quills necessary for that migration may be moulted there.

Like the young storm petrel, the fledgeling shearwater is fat and heavier than its parents when they cease to feed and visit it—at much the same age in both—around the sixtieth day of its life. The large and lethargic young shearwater certainly needs a period of fasting, and hardening of its flight feathers, to achieve the dangerous journey from an inland burrow to the sea. Even then, except on a night of high wind which assists take-off, its progress is no more than a fluttering walk or scramble along the ground, surmounting obstacles with the help of its hooked bill, clawed feet and beating wings. But first it exercises its wings, which it has not been able to do in the narrow confines of the burrow. This it does by night when, a few days after its last feed and now losing weight steadily, it makes its first appearance above ground. One is entitled to imagine what is hard to prove: that it must be hungry or thirsty, or both, and that this may be an additional inspiration to bring it forth. But there it is, suddenly emerged and squatting close to the burrow entrance. At last it is able to flap its wings without hindrance.

The young shearwater does so for perhaps half an hour on the first midnight sally, then just as suddenly it shuffles head-first back to the hidden dark nest where it was born. It is too inexperienced and unsteady on its weak legs even to walk. (Neither shearwater nor storm petrel when normally at rest stand upright, as depicted in older bird books; their legs are placed too far to the rear of the body.) It is a dangerous moment, for if by chance it is blown by a strong wind away from the burrow entrance, it may not be able to find its way back, or find a suitable hiding place before dawn, when the resident gulls, buzzards, ravens and carrion crows begin their morning search for food. At this autumn season on Skokholm, when each night hundreds of fledgeling shearwaters are emerging and exercising their wings, a proportion fail to make the sea, or adequate cover; the period of this exodus is a time of feasting for the predatory birds.

However, this slaughter of the helpless innocents has not in the present century had dire results on the total population. Both shearwater and storm-petrel numbers at Skokholm have in fact greatly increased, more than doubled since my estimates made fifty years ago. Although those early estimates were undoubtedly too conservative, there has been a vast increase, which could be put down locally to human protection, and the cessation of farming operations which has left the fields and hedge-walls available for

Predatory great black-backed gull with Manx shearwater

burrowing. In the case of the shearwater it has spread to occupy burrows formerly used by the puffins, which have greatly declined in numbers—for reasons which are not clear, but one of these must be the all-too-frequent oil pollution from the new industrial complex of the Milford Haven oil-terminal wharves and refineries, which you may see starkly smoking upon the eastern horizon opposite Skokholm.

It is not so easy to explain the doubling and trebling of the island's storm-petrel population in the same period, except as part of a general increase of this petrel throughout its breeding range on islands off western British coasts. But that general increase needs explaining too; possibly it is partly because shearwater, storm petrel and most of the smaller related tubenosed species seem to be able to avoid contact with the many slicks of crude oil which trouble the seas of the world. They are birds that fly much more than they swim, and as they are now known to have a keen sense of smell, they may well deliberately avoid strong-smelling pools of inedible oil floating on the sea. But diving birds such as puffin, razorbill, guillemot and sea-ducks, which are frequently washed ashore dying or dead from the effects of oiled plumage, and which are flightless during the period of the annual moult of wing quills at sea, are at all times thereby more vulnerable, more liable to swim into contact with the oil.

At this autumn season I would enjoy a quiet September midnight studying the behaviour of the fledgelings, and of any visiting adults, at the shearwater burrows and storm-petrel crevices. Periods of moonlight were of course easier for observation, although it was not difficult, except on nights of black cloud, to watch the individual in the twilight of a moonless night with a clear sky. The human eye gradually adjusts from artificial light to see reasonably well outdoors in the diminished light; and a spotlight torch was used, but only briefly, to assist in locating the source of bird movement within a few paces of the observer.

There are many references in ornithologial literature to a marked tendency of the smaller tubenosed species which are nocturnal in visiting the land to do so more freely and in larger numbers on moonless nights. The most popular reason given is 'fear' of predators which, normally diurnal, can see more clearly and will actively hunt and kill these petrels then, or at least those which attract attention by blundering movements on the ground near the sleeping places or nests of the predators (gulls, skuas). In his interesting paper, Imber (1975) advances the alternative view that lesser numbers visiting their breeding grounds on moonlit nights than on darker nights are probably the results of poor feeding conditions; fish prey he suggests do not come so near the surface of the sea on moonlit nights. (Most of us have seen so-called phosphorescence at sea in a ship's wake at night. This is caused by luminescent plankton—on which storm petrels feed.) He adds what is certainly true: that fledgeling petrels are particularly liable to be attracted to artificial lights situated near the breeding colony. I have several times had to rescue fledgeling shearwaters (Skokholm, Skomer and at two New Zealand colonies) from death when they have fluttered into a bright camp-fire during their midnight sally from burrow to sea. Shearwaters and storm petrels frequently strike the lantern of lighthouses on dark nights— but then so do many other birds. Imber concludes: 'It is suggested that nocturnal-feeding petrels are instinctively attracted to light sources because they exploit bioluminescent prey. A small proportion of fledgelings seem to be initially misled by this instinct.' The bright spotlight of our torch beamed upon the head of shearwater or storm petrel disconcerted the bird, and the shearwater might move away; if it was a newly emerged fledgeling shearwater, however, it seldom did so, but sat quietly, eyes blinking at first, or head turned aside. But any storm petrel, discovered at rest in the open, was only momentarily confused: within seconds it had flown off. It was rare for me to be nimble enough to catch one by hand or in a handnet.

It will be opportune to note here that other, non-human, observers were encountered at night, likewise searching for petrels entering or leaving their nest-holes. At Skokholm each winter an influx of little owls (*Athene noctua*) resulted in some years in a pair remaining to breed; and if so, they found it convenient to perch at night close to storm-petrel nesting sites. When an

Little owl with British storm petrel

adult petrel flew in from the sea, the owl could easily pounce upon it silently, just at the moment—no more than two or three seconds—when the petrel was folding its wings at the entrance to its narrow nest-hole. That this was a profitable moment for securing prey was evident when one day in July 1936 we found a nest of this owl in a rabbit burrow, with two owl chicks and a larder of nearly 200 corpses of storm petrels, the majority with only the head removed! We caught and deported the owl family, and in future adopted a policy of shooting or banishing this owl from Skokholm, preferring to protect our petrels rather than encourage this acclimatised importation from Europe. A second owl was the short-eared species (*Asio flammeus*) which, although not nesting on Skokholm, would occasionally fly over the sea from Skomer, 4 kilometres distant, and raid our storm-petrel colonies. These visitors were probably immature owls or failed breeders with no nesting cares, who sojourned for a while on our island; they would be flushed by day from a roosting place in the central *Molinia* marsh, where they left the evidence of this nocturnal predation in the form of owl pellets containing storm-petrel feathers and bones.

From this experience of watching adult storm petrels entering or leaving the nest-hole, we were not too surprised to find that the young petrel, emerging for the first time, did not linger, like the fledgeling shearwater, gaze around and at the stars, then return to the safety of the burrow after an interval of time; instead, on the very few occasions when it was possible to be

Short-eared owl over Skokholm

present when a fledgeling emerged (my records give only four instances), it flew away within ten seconds. This almost instant departure flight raised a number of queries, as well as admiration that this little sea bird could fly from the warm darkness of the nest straight into the cold windy world of the boisterous autumn ocean, with no experience even of exercising its wings. Often this exodus occurred after the equinox, on cool nights at the end of September and in October with occasional departures in November.

One could understand better the more cautious approach to the sea made by the fledgeling shearwaters. From frequent handling earlier in the earth burrows so conveniently outside our back door, these young birds were almost tame, hardly perturbed at all when we sat within a pace or two of them on these nights of emergence. The deserted, plump, black-coated creatures continued to occupy turf seats just outside their burrows each night for up to their seventy-fourth day of existence, before each flapped away to the sea. They had been deserted about the sixtieth day, had remained fasting below ground for three or four days, then had indulged, sensibly, in wing-exercises outside for another five to seven nights. I could understand how important this was. The problem of their migration lay ahead, a riddle to me but one which the youngster would surmount, despite a little sympathetic worry and wonder on my part. But how did they do it? At such a tender age, and without guidance from the adults, long departed, how did they know what to do, which way to fly, how to obtain food? Watching, recording, staring and pondering—the overall mystery was beyond the capacity of my understanding. To me, such words as automatic, instinct, innate, were inadequate to explain these complicated patterns of behaviour carried out so perfectly by young creatures with no visual or other guidance from parents or other adults. The words explained nothing, and yet this initial behaviour which ensured the survival of the species, although seemingly intelligent, was not intelligent at all—according to most students of animal behaviour.

Squatting beside my squatting young shearwater at night I had ample time to observe and converse with this pigeon-sized bird, which made no vocal response, unless you count the audible winnowing of its wings at frequent intervals. This action at times lifted it to the very tips of its webbed toes. 'Of what indeed are you thinking, young *Puffinus*?' my thoughts would run. 'Are you hungry? Thirsty? Do you realise that your parents at this moment are far away, winging southwards across the Bay of Biscay, feeding on the sardines which shoal in great masses from Spain north in summer to the English Channel? I know, because some of the shearwaters marked at Skokholm are from time to time shot by Basque and Breton fishermen. They write to report any recoveries of our banded ones; and some expect a monetary reward, not just an acknowledgement of the scientific importance of the record. They eat them, after they have opened the birds' stomachs to ascertain how lately they have taken sardines, so the fishermen can set their nets accordingly.

'But of course, I forget, you have never seen your parents, or any other bird—another shearwater, a puffin or a rabbit—which may have visited your birth-burrow while you were still a dependent infant. How stupid of me! All you can have learned in your short life of two months is the voice and touch of your parents bringing you warmth, food and a familiar talk which you will—or ought to—remember with pleasure for all your life. When my enquiring hand lifted the sod lid above the nest at the end of the burrow and admitted the blinding light of day you did not bite my fingers at first. You were too young, and to me very beautiful in your smooth double down, so that I was impelled to stroke you, and murmur soothing noises of admiration. But later, as you shed that down and grew the beginnings of that resplendent black-and-white plumage, you became aggressive, and bit my hand quite severely.'

Between bouts of wing-exercise the young shearwater preened a lot, tweaking with its long bill the oil gland (situated above the 'parson's nose' which holds the tail quills) and transferring the oil to all parts of its new feathers. To oil the back of its head, this was rubbed against the gland, and then the oiled crown feathers combed with the clawed foot to spread the oil down the neck and upper back which the beak could not reach. Although the young storm petrel was too quick to leave its nest crevice for observation of wing-flapping or preening activities at the moment of its departure, doubtless in the burrow it frequently preened, like the young shearwater, and oiled its feathers in the way well-grown nestlings of all species do before fledging. Full-length wing-flapping is rarely possible within the confines of a storm-petrel burrow, but small exercises are carried out. I have watched a well-feathered storm-petrel chick stretch one wing backwards in line with the leg on that side of the body. This was in a very shallow nest-hole in the rocks of Little Bay cliffs, well lit during the day.

Wing-flapping and preening: what other activity did the fledgeling shearwater enjoy, sitting on its outdoor night couch of grass and thrift in front of the burrow? Very rarely it might rest its bill for a moment in a sleeping position, sunk upon its breast or the back of its wing; but most of the time its head was held well up, in a watchful attitude, slowly but fairly constantly moving from side to side, and now and then tilted upwards as if it were looking at the stars. Gazing in fact, much as I gazed: at intervals listening and looking around for signs of other creatures in the half-light, and frequently studying the sky. Out of long habit as an amateur astronomer I would first orientate by the Pole Star, easily found in the clear sky by the 'pointers' of the Plough. But in those early sessions by night with my young shearwaters I did not attach any significance to the possibility that their imminent migration might be guided by the celestial signs; that in gazing at the heavens so often the fledgeling was 'imprinting' upon its memory-cells a chart of the positions of the major fixed stars as at that hour and night of the month above its birthplace. All I might have thought was that the young bird, when later it was ready to breed, like any other bird and most animals, might remember the surroundings where it was born, and head for home with the intention of finding a familiar territory in which to locate a partner and initiate the nesting process. Banding studies of many species of land birds at that time had already indicated that in general this is what happened; to return home was a natural insurance to maintain the numbers of a species in its proper ecological environment.

It was enough, at this early stage of only two or three years of somewhat casual observation, to record accurately their physical movements and how at last the young shearwater, considerably thinner and with well-exercised strengthened wings, flapped away downhill and blundered over the cliffs to the safety of the sea. In a strong wind it might be airborne at the cliff edge, but it was not yet used to long flight, and would soon hit the sea.

What happened when it did touch the water I was many times able to observe, by taking down to the sea by day any young shearwaters which had failed to reach it during the night, and which I was able to pick up in the open before predatory birds had attacked them. Thrown from my hand as I stood a few metres above the sea, they invariably flapped downwards, not one making a clear getaway on the wing.

The first reactions of a healthy young shearwater on folding its wings at the surface was to swim a little, and sip water thirstily. It was soon spotted by the numerous gulls nesting on the island, and they invariably swooped upon it; the young shearwater dived in good time to avoid being caught by a death-dealing bill. Using its half-open wings like paddle-wheels, it swam away to sea under the water, coming up for air some distance away. It dived again if the gulls attacked once more; but usually the gulls soon gave up the fruitless attempts. Only when a fledgeling was sick and thin (fledgeling shearwaters sometimes suffered from a debilitating epizootic disease causing conjunctivitis and blistered feet) did it fail to escape to sea when we released it by day. It might have difficulty, being so light, in diving, or lack normal co-ordination of wing and leg movement; these feeble unfortunates would be at once attacked and killed as they floated upon the surface. We therefore learned to release them in the sea by night, the normal time for fledgelings to depart. This inability of the fledgeling shearwater to fly on reaching the sea for the first time, is in great contrast to the fledgeling behaviour of our storm petrel, as already described.

6
The long migration

It is reasonably argued that the migration of birds and other animals of the land, including caribou and other deer, butterflies and certain other insects, and at sea many species of cetaceans and fishes, was encouraged in the first place by the several (probably four) glaciations which occurred during the last 100,000 years. At the height of each glaciation the polar ice-caps advanced several hundred kilometres towards the equator, destroying animals and plants that were unable to escape. However, these advances were apparently gradual and there was time for most species, even of some sedentary plants and animals, to survive by successive generations retreating from the cold and ice towards the equator.

Some mobile species were able to adapt better than others to the colder conditions at the more temperate limits of the glaciation, so long as food was available. In summer they (especially birds and whales) could follow this food supply moving towards the pole, as they do today. Thus some of these initiated the habit of long-distance migration. In the storm petrels less than half the species are long-distance migrants; the others, chiefly tropical and sub-tropical petrels, have remained or become sedentary, finding their feeding niche close to home at all seasons.

Some 10,000 years ago, when the most recent amelioration of world climate set in, the ice-caps gradually retreated to reach their present limits, resulting in the ocean levels rising approximately 100 metres to their present height. This submerged much land; Britain separated from Europe when the sea flooded through to form the Straits of Dover; Tasmania was separated from Australia, and New Zealand split into three main islands. There was a return of certain hardy species to establish or re-establish breeding grounds in high latitudes, as we know them today. As regards storm petrels, in Chapter 10 we examine the astonishing life-history of the hardiest species of all, the smallest Antarctic sea bird, Wilson's petrel, which rears its chick in burrows often covered with snow; yet makes one of the longest migrations of all.

Our *Hydrobates pelagicus* is now proved, by over a thousand recoveries at home and abroad of marked individuals, to migrate southwards at the end of the breeding season, passing along the sea-coasts both sides of Britain and Ireland, into the Bay of Biscay. The bulk of this migration has moved on

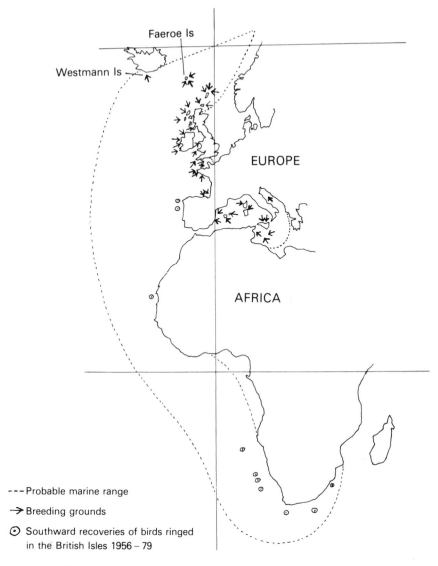

Faeroe Is

Westmann Is

EUROPE

AFRICA

- - - Probable marine range

→ Breeding grounds

⊙ Southward recoveries of birds ringed
in the British Isles 1956 – 79

Breeding grounds and marine range of the British storm petrel

down the western Iberian shore before the end of the year. From November
to January many are seen (and one or more banded individuals have been
recovered) off Mauretania and the west coast of Africa north of the equator.
Specimens collected in midwinter off these coasts, and now in Dutch
museums, were all juveniles a few months old. These young petrels, hardly
as strong-winged as their parents, probably find congenial winter quarters
in the warm tropical seas off West Africa. But the experienced breeding
adults travel much further south, cross the equatorial doldrums, and reach

the latitude of the Tropic of Capricorn in the region of the coast of Namibia. Here the cool Benguela Current sweeps north from its far Antarctic origin, a turbulent mass of water rich in planktonic food, diverted by the southern thrust of the Cape of Good Hope. At this windy corner of Africa there is much upwelling where the warm Indian Ocean current mingles with the cold billows of the Atlantic side. Between Namibia and Natal is one of the richest commercial fisheries in the world.

By the time the adult storm petrels arrive during November and December the southern hemisphere summer is well advanced. Wisely they have omitted the chill northern winter from their lives; and indeed as long as they shall live they will not know the rigours of either northern or southern winter. They will live in perpetual summer, migrating from the autumn in the northern hemisphere to late spring and early summer in the southern hemisphere, and vice-versa. The presence of British storm petrels off these coasts of South Africa in numbers during the northern winter has been known for many decades (van Oordt & Kruijt, 1953), but not where they originated from until, thanks to extensive banding in Britain, six marked individuals have been, and more may soon be, recorded there. These include adults from Skokholm. An astonishingly long sea voyage for such a tiny sea bird! The distance between this petrel's most northerly known breeding colonies just south of the Arctic Circle on the Westmann Islands (South Iceland) and on the Lofoten Isles off Norway, and the Cape of Good Hope, following the shortest great circle route over the sea (roughly the longitude 20°W) as far south as the equator, then a line south-east to the Cape of Good Hope (on the 20°E meridian) is approximately 14,000 kilometres; and for the individual petrels which have entered the Indian Ocean and reached the Natal coast, we can add another 1,200 kilometres. Say an average total migratory journey of over 30,000 kilometres annually for each fully adult breeding British storm petrel; but this is only a chart-reading of the straight-line or surface distance travelled. During the wavering flight and erratic feeding movements the actual distance covered in flight by this little bird might safely be trebled to a minimum of 100,000 kilometres of ocean-wandering annually!

Recoveries of marked storm petrels are usually of individuals washed or blown ashore dying or dead, evidently exhausted during onshore gales; but a number are caught alive on board ship at night, attracted by artificial light. One British storm petrel flew into my cabin through the open port-hole of a liner in the Bay of Biscay one night in August 1939. In the same summer a Bulwer's petrel (*Bulweria bulwerii*) alighted beside me as I lay resting on the deck of a small steamer on a calm night north of the Canary Islands. (This is not a true storm petrel, but is almost twice as large, a handsome bird which in that year I had been studying on small islands south of Madeira.)

Finding the Route

The riddle of how the fledgeling storm petrel or any other lone young migrant bird guides its migration to keep within the traditional route to the wintering ground is fascinating, and the subject of continuing speculation and experiment. Why, for example, do our Skokholm shearwaters—both adult and young—make a rapid transequatorial flight to reach the eastern coast of South America, as far south as Patagonia, escaping winter to enjoy life in the southern summer? Whereas our storm petrels, flying the same southward route at about the same time through the Bay of Biscay, on passing West Africa turn south and south-east to reach the South African coast.

Generally, ocean-wandering birds seem to take advantage of prevailing winds, and it has been stated that the course of their migration is much influenced, if not controlled, by the trade winds. Due to the west-to-east rotation of the earth, these circulate in a clockwise direction immediately north of the equator, and anti-clockwise immediately south thereof. In the sub-Antarctic latitudes, around 60°S, with no land masses to intercept it, the prevailing wind blows west to east fiercely, dragging with it the chill ice-laden, Antarctic surface water, circling unhindered around the outer limits of the Antarctic continent. The northern limits of this eastward flow of water, popularly known as the Roaring Forties, are deflected north by the south-western walls of South America (the Humboldt Current), of South Africa (the Benguela Current), and of Australia. These wind-whipped turbulent seas provide rich ocean feeding-grounds by the upwelling of nutrient minerals and salts which nourish the phytoplanktonic base of the living ocean food chain, as already described. The stronger the movement of the surface water under persistent gales, the stronger must be this upwelling effect of the benthic counter-current flowing close to the bed of the sea below. But strong winds (although not those of hurricane force), also assist sea-bird travellers in their feeding and migratory movements, by giving lift both to hover in the air, and to fly at speed, with less effort of wing-beating. The albatrosses, with the longest wings of any bird, inhabit only the windiest latitudes of the world, where they are able to glide with scarcely a flap of the wings for hours and days—save in rare calms when they may be obliged to rest on the sea.

Each migrant is conditioned—we do not yet understand how—to fly to its traditional wintering ground: Manx shearwaters fly to the coasts of Brazil and Argentina, British storm petrels to the windy plankton-rich seas around the Cape of Good Hope; the Antarctic-nesting Wilson's storm petrel migrates north to winter—in summer there—in the fertile upwelling waters of the North Atlantic; the European swallow escapes the northern winter by migrating to live in the South African summer (some even in the villages and towns, in sight of our storm petrels close offshore). The direction of the trade winds which migrating shearwaters from Skokholm encounter, on their route across the equator to South America, is generally helpful; so why do both species of our adult storm petrels, far weaker and slower on the wing, deviate when they reach the West African coast in the autumn? The smaller bird heads into opposing winds all the way south by east to the Namibian coast and Cape of Good Hope feeding grounds. Studying the chart it is difficult to find adequate oceanographic reasons; and again only speculation remains.

It was in the hope that a related problem—of how birds are able to orientate and find their way over what is to man a featureless desert of water—that a series of homing experiments with sea birds was initiated at Skokholm in 1936; these were continued, somewhat desultorily, when the island bird observatory was reopened there after the 1939–45 war. The species we chose in the first tests were Manx shearwater, storm petrel and puffin. These were considered to be ideal because they were accessible in burrows for marking, release and subsequent recapture, using only incubating birds, which were most likely to return home swiftly, having the incentive of resuming incubation duty with a life partner. Of the three species, only the shearwater proved satisfactory, from its comparative tameness and tolerance of handling in its burrow. Storm petrel and puffin both deserted too readily, and were therefore not sent away on the longer distances in these experiments. Of those storm petrels and puffins which did return from release points on coasts within 300 kilometres of Skokholm, individual breeding birds did so rapidly enough to suggest that as soon as they were released they 'knew' in which direction to fly home.

But the strong-winged shearwaters, whose transequatorial migration at that time (1936) was not proven by banding returns, made swift passages home from distances as far as Boston, Massachussetts, North America (4,800km), and Venice (1,496km) at the head of the almost landlocked Adriatic Sea. It must be noted that in all these experiments a proportion of the individuals of the three species were not recovered at their nests again— not necessarily because they never returned; some 'non-recoveries' were undoubtedly due to humans failing to maintain a constant watch. If we analyse the published results of these and other sea-bird homing experiments, they do no more than prove that some individuals of long-distance migratory species, when displaced far out of their normal sea-range, have this capability to find their way home at speeds which preclude random searching. We may argue that they must be guided by an inbuilt knowledge of which way to fly; again not (as we perhaps arrogantly refuse to believe) by intelligent reasoning, as man defines conceptual thought. Nevertheless, despite that definition, we still do not know how long-distance migrants navigate with such speed and accuracy. The most acceptable explanation, and one which may also explain why each species follows a traditional migration route (shearwaters from Skokholm to and from South America, and storm petrels to and from South Africa), is that they are guided by an inbuilt knowledge of celestial navigation, which is their equivalent of man's learned knowledge of how to navigate by modern direction—and position-finding instruments: chronometer, compass, sextant, chart and trigonometric tables.

For its chronometer the bird has an accurate time-sense by which it regulates its twenty-four-hour routine by the changing position of the sun and its light by day; and, if active nocturnally, by the (apparently) fixed and changing positions of the moon, stars and planets in the night sky. The same sense of time must play a part in seasonal movements. Most if not all animals have this precise sense of time, although in sophisticated urban-dwelling man, governed by the mechanical clock, it is atrophied through disuse. However, primitive peoples who live in close contact with nature and have no such mechanical aids retain a strong sense of time, consciously or unconsciously, aware of its passage as the sun by day and the major stars and the moon by night move in their orbits in the sky. Even without additional guidance from landscape and objects on land, the Polynesian and Micronesian seafaring people used to make regular and accurate inter-island voyages over the Pacific for hundreds of miles without sight of land. They were taught how to steer, without compass, by the position of the celestial bodies, supplemented—in case of fog or mist obscuring the heavens—by a knowledge of local winds and currents.

But dense fog during calm windless weather confuses both man and bird. Unable to see the sun or stars, and with no directional wind to lift wing or sail, migration is halted. Birds and man at sea may fish for food to support life during such weather, but it has many times been proved that birds cease to migrate during dead calms when the celestial guides are totally obscured. Migrating sea birds can rest on the sea, but land birds caught by heavy windless mist at sea must keep flying or perish by drowning. They have, however, the alternative of ascending above the mist (and many land-breeding birds migrate regularly at heights of up to 1,000 metres), when they can reorientate on sighting the sun or stars again. Low-flying birds, confused in fog, will fly towards any bright light: many are killed against the lanterns of lighthouses during migration when overtaken by dense mist. These include shearwaters and petrels, which are not known to fly normally more than about 50 metres—usually very much less—above the sea.

So much for that small dark eye of the lone fledgeling storm petrel to learn! So much information for its brain and cerebral cortex to take in to ensure its survival when it emerges from burrow darkness to see those heavenly guides for the first time. But how does this wonderful camera of the eye set its inbuilt chronometer-compass-sextant to work?

In lowly animals such as the fruit-fly *Drosophila*, experiments have shown that a first flash of light during the larval stage is necessary to set the inbuilt biological clock ticking; if deprived of light while developing from egg to adult, its time-sense is disorganised, and it may emerge as a perfect fly too late to survive. In this species the adult needs to emerge just before dawn in order to take advantage of the hour of greatest humidity in which its tender tiny body can absorb sufficient moisture and at the same time toughen its water-resistant skin against the drying heat of the sun. The infant shearwater or petrel may receive little or no clear flash of light through the narrow, often winding, tunnel to its birth-nest; but when at last it emerges it must be able to adjust the untried biological clock to synchronise with the night hours when it first gazes at the starlit heavens. But while the fledgeling shearwater, as we have seen, has several consecutive nights, each of an hour or two, to study—if it does—the position of the major fixed stars wheeling clockwise around Polaris, the fixed North Star, our emergent storm petrel tarries not a minute, but is off to sea in haste. It is as if it never looked at the sky, but it nevertheless navigates just as expertly as its larger cousin.

The Driving Force

The ticking timekeeper in the small brain of our fledgeling storm petrel warns it to emerge about the sixtieth day, but always and only at night; and on untested wings to fly immediately to the sea. When sufficiently far from the dangers of the land, it will soon need to feed (although the moment for this will depend on how much reserve fat it carries). It will navigate correctly without the guidance of its parents along the traditional route of its species. Studying this behaviour, the next query which arose was: what is the driving force or physiological state that compels a migrant to undertake long journeys?

The impulse to migrate is evidently as innate as the bird's ability to navigate. I have observed night-migrant warblers which had been caught on their southward autumn migration and experimentally caged at Heligoland Island bird observatory, Germany. They exhibited an intense restlessness, for a few hours of complete darkness, before and after midnight, wing-beating and fidgeting on their perches. These had been coupled by an electronic device to a time-graph which measured and recorded every vibration of the perches caused by the activity of the restless migrants. Before dawn this activity ceased and the birds fell asleep in the darkness. They had lost much weight during the exercise and needed to feed well during the next day to stay alive. If released at night during this intense period of restlessness these small nocturnal migrants dart away into the darkness, and are lost to sight as they rise up into the sky and resume their migration. When this fever is on them they can no more stop migrating than stop breathing. Normally in the evening before starting this night activity the tiny bundle of feathers which is a warbler is plump with enough fat reserves, built up by heavy feeding all day, to last through the night; but it uses up this fuel rapidly during the hours of flying through cold night air.

This knowledge, of innate restlessness to migrate, enables us to understand better why the plump storm-petrel fledgeling is impelled, at a given moment of physiological readiness (which must be mental as well as hormonal), to escape from the land and perhaps for hours beat its wings joyously—if instinctively—in the new freedom of air and ocean, gathering greater strength with practice, and sustained by the fat reserves laid on in the nest.

A Waterproof Coat

In birds, fat is stored largely within the abdominal cavity and attached to the viscera; as required it is dissolved and conveyed as vital blood through the arteries, where it supplies energy, by oxidation in the muscle cells, to operate the flying machine. In the petrel, as we have seen, fat in the form of oil secreted by the walls of the stomach has other uses: it is ejected through the mouth at intruders at the nest or when a petrel is handled by man. It forms much of the warm semi-digested soup regurgitated by the parent to feed the chick in the first week or two before more solid food is supplied. A similar oil, secreted from the gland above the tail, is used in preening and waterproofing every part of the plumage.

So oily and fat is the nestling petrel that, before the advent of paraffin lighting oil, its body was used as a primitive form of lamp by island-dwelling people of the Hebrides and Faeroe Islands, accustomed to harvesting sea birds for food. A thread of some material (wool or a dried rush) was passed through the corpse, the oil burning well on this wick, if rather sootily. Or the oil was squeezed from the fresh carcase into a container—to be used for domestic purposes; the latter method is still employed by some of the Maori 'muttonbirders' when harvesting the young 'titi' (fledgelings of the smaller burrowing tubenose species such as prions and white-faced storm petrels) on the off-islands of New Zealand.

Thus well equipped with fuel for the long migration, our storm petrel will nevertheless need to feed sooner and more often than the great albatrosses. Their large bodies and leisurely soaring gliding flight conserve energy, and lose internal heat (= energy = fat) less rapidly than the little Mother Carey petrels, whose almost ceaseless rapid wing-beating and twisting flight require a proportionately larger and more frequent recharging of the metabolic batteries.

Arrival at Winter Quarters

The contrast between the flight and behaviour at sea of the largest and smallest of the tubenoses may be seen and admired at their common rendezvous off the southern tip of Africa. The long narrow arm of the Cape of Good Hope is a provincial nature reserve and wild-animal park, a rocky peninsula with ample space for a selection of harmless native animals— wildebeest, zebra, baboon, various species of antelope, springbok, etc—to roam and breed freely. Native flowering plants adapted to the windy climate adorn the headland with rich colours. It is pleasant to sit, as we have, at the end of this promontory, and observe the considerable passage and feeding movements of oceanic birds. These are best seen on a day of moderate wind; in a dead calm the sea birds tend to fly farther offshore.

On your right, to the west, is the Atlantic Ocean, cooled by the Benguela Current. To your left and south-east across the deep indent of False Bay, Cape Agulhas is some 180km distant, the farthest south headland of Africa,

Wandering albatross glides above dipping storm petrels

Giant petrel with Cape pigeons off the Cape of Good Hope

bathed in the warm Indian Ocean current sweeping south-west from the Mozambique Channel. Here, between and around the two great capes, waters of two temperatures clash with great turbulence for several hundred kilometres extending offshore. It is possibly the best place in the world to observe storm petrels dipping and flitting in typical erratic flight, feet frequently pattering over the waves while at the same moment the world's largest albatross *Diomedea exulans*, the wanderer with the wingspan of nearly 11ft (3.35m), glides close overhead.

My first visit was during the southern summer, just after the solstice and Christmas time. A gentle south-easterly breeze gave lift to the wings of innumerable birds feeding or migrating as far as the eye could see, from the white surf below our cliff perch to the grey-blue landless southern horizon. The Cape pigeon *Daption capense* was the most numerous tubenose in sight; but the giant petrel, dark and forbidding with its heavy bill (occasionally a pure white individual may be seen) was a visible second in numbers; by its graceful gliding flight it should not be confused with the more lumbering gull-like but equally dark and predatory great skua. Both nest on sub-Antarctic islands, and those we saw at that moment were almost certainly immature, non-breeding individuals.

Local black-backed and silver gulls, and terns, mingled with a few of the world's record long-distance migrant, the graceful Arctic tern, at that

Arctic terns migrating

moment in somewhat ragged moult; they too were probably immatures born barely six months ago in the high northern latitude nesting places. Like our adult storm petrels, the parent terns make a longer migration to the south, and, according to Salomonsen (1967), from the evidence of banding records and observation at sea, some of these hardy tireless older birds drift eastwards on the wind around the whole Antarctic continent during the southern summer, completing this circumnavigation (and their annual moult) in time to start north again in March and April. Close inshore we saw jackass penguins, swimming typically low in the water, and diving often; they breed on small islands near the Cape. And resting or running about on the rocks above the tide-line were handsome turnstones, waders born in the high Arctic. Our sea- and shore-bird list was formidable; it included the black oystercatcher of the Cape, sleeping on one leg on a pinnacle of rock while the tide was high; and long lines and chevrons of gannets and cormorants were stringing past. But some were fishing. The gannets now and then amused us by their spectacular diving plunge, trailing the wings in a diagonal which is last to vanish in the explosion of white water. Two white-headed fish eagles flew past.

When the eye had become accustomed to the dark serrated pattern of wave-shadows, it was possible to pick out the smallest birds a quarter of a mile away, the storm petrels. Not easy to be sure which one of two species you may see at the Cape; it is best to mount a good telescope on a tripod here to ensure a close-up view. Depending on the season you may see more of one than the other. Both are equally great travellers, and they meet at the Cape in the southern hemisphere midsummer. In Chapter 10 we deal with the remarkable Wilson's storm petrel, the mature adults of which were at that midsummer moment nesting in the coldest part of their ocean range, the Antarctic mainland and its ice-capped islands. These individuals mingling with our northern storm petrels, sharing the rich Cape planktonic food that day, were therefore youngsters of up to three years, not yet old enough to breed, content to live in a summer of ease alongside their adult British cousins. Even under the telescope they are very alike externally. White of rump, in size almost identical. But the practised eye soon discovers differences. Most marked is the wing-action: the more rounded wings of the Wilson's petrel carry it with a more sweeping swallow-like flight, except when it is hovering or lightly walking on the surface. Then if you are close enough you see the yellow panels in the upper webs of its longer legs—these two differences are quite distinctive: the Wilson's is, you say to yourself, just that much darker and slightly bigger as well. This darkness is emphasised when the all-black under-wing catches your eye; our northern storm petrel in flight exhibits a distinct white streak or bar under its wing.

Jackass penguins

How far south beyond the Cape does our Skokholm bird fly? Lambert (1971) records it present at 38°S, 399km south of Cape Agulhas, well into the main stream of migration of the once numerous whales and dolphins, now alas much reduced by overhunting. Visiting the Cape Point Reserve headland with friends on two occasions in the southern spring (29 September and 20 October) we failed to locate any British storm petrels among the rather fewer sea birds feeding or migrating past. They had not yet arrived. But once more the eye was caught by the beauty and ease of the long-winged great albatrosses. Although their nearest nesting grounds are in the Tristan da Cunha group and other remote, more sub-Antarctic islands, perhaps a few thousand kilometres from the Cape of Good Hope, the distance home on those swift-gliding wings, which easily overtake the fastest ship, is a matter of hours rather than days. But some of these *exulans* wanderers at the Cape are not yet out of their dark juvenile plumage—they do not achieve the pure white underparts of the adult dress until they are about ten years old. And even when fully adult the larger *Diomedea* albatrosses, it is now discovered, take so long in incubating the egg and rearing the solitary chick that they do not mate and nest in the following year.

In their adolescent, and sabbatical or off-duty adult years, the great albatrosses are free to wander the world. They prefer to keep within the windiest parts of their range. Some, like the wandering and giant petrel species, easing their long wings upon the gales of the Roaring Forties, perform a circumnavigation of the globe in that latitude, pausing to feed where cold currents from the Antarctic move north in turbulence against the extremities of the southern continents. Banding returns have helped to prove this circumnavigation, just as they are helping to elucidate the movements of our storm petrels so far south. At present we know that the majority of adult storm petrels which winter there leave the Cape feeding grounds in March and April, and will not return before November or December.

Just a few of these petrels have been recorded at the Cape in May and early June, so late that it is obvious that they are either not fully mature and ready to breed, or are rare instances of individual established breeders enjoying a sabbatical summer. Or, since death must overtake us all, are they old, as old as a storm petrel can be, and no longer willing or able to undertake the long laborious voyage home?

7
The return home

Banding of many thousands of British storm petrels has revealed a fascinating, hitherto unsuspected, aspect of their behaviour at sea. It has been discovered that they are perhaps the most erratic of all wandering birds during their years of youthful freedom before they take up the serious business of reproduction.

Up to 1953, before Peter Davis launched his study at Skokholm in 1954, only 1,723 British storm petrels had been banded, chiefly at Skokholm. Few of these were nestlings. But in the next twenty-seven years well over 70,000 were banded, most of them along the west coasts of Wales, Scotland and Ireland, with smaller numbers as far north as the Faeroe Islands, and south to the Channel Islands and Brittany. Of this large number over 1,000 recoveries are available for analysis, producing a fairly clear picture of the movements of individuals, from the year of birth to that of effective breeding, and into old age. Late in this period Antony R. Mainwood (1976–81) and his assistants have probably banded more storm petrels than

British storm petrels returning home

anyone else, and it has been our privilege to have helped on some of his midsummer mist-netting nights in the Hebrides. It is largely from his devoted work and inspiration in the field, on remote islands and cliffs, that we are able to draw the story unfolded in this chapter.

From the preceding chapters on arrival, breeding and departure at Skokholm, it is clear that the storm petrel does not have a closely synchronised nesting season. Egg production in most species of bird is timed to take advantage of the period of optimum food availability for the female to build the egg. Perhaps because the weather is often bad in the northern spring, and sea food at times scarce, egg-laying in our petrel is spread over several weeks: the extreme dates from Skokholm records are 28 May and 16 July; resulting in a similar wide spacing of fledging dates, between the last week of September and the first week of November. It is probable that the very late instances are due to first laying by a young female, or else that the first egg of a mature female was lost and a second one laid. Replacement eggs are rare, but (of six known) between fifteen and thirty days elapsed between loss and relaying (page 42).

Whether they are early or late in breeding, the successful parents usually cease to visit their fat fully-feathered fledgeling several days before it is ready to leave the nest-crevice. Banding returns of these adults indicate that they do not tarry, but hasten south on that long voyage across the equator to the southern midsummer, described in the last chapter. It is a long journey there and back, yet marking of mated pairs proves that with rare exceptions, as long as both shall live, they meet again each summer at the familiar nesting place, to renew their partnership and, in the dark warm crevice which is their marriage bed, utter their purring vows of faithfulness to one another.

It would be nice to believe that the mated pair are sufficiently attached to each other by voice recognition to call and come together at sea, where the bright light of day will assist sight recognition; and that they will migrate together as a result. But there is no evidence, by observation, or recovery of a marked pair together on migration, that any of the tubenosed family remain close together after nesting has finished. Wild swans and geese fly in family groups together on migration, and mate for life; puffins and other auks seem to associate in pairs outside their burrow or rock homes, and some call to each other and mate on the sea below the nesting cliffs, but there is no evidence that these diving sea birds remain close together during the winter migration. On the contrary, most storm petrels encountered at sea are noted to be solitary, except when temporarily concentrated at a food source. This solitariness may be occasioned by the need to disperse widely and fly low over the waves to find the small organisms of their diet.

White-fronted geese migrating in a family party

The Annual Moult

Seasonal physiological changes taking place almost suddenly at the end of the breeding season induce migrant animals to undertake their traditional migrations. The annual moult in birds imposes a particular strain upon their metabolism. Certain species of ground-living land birds drop their feathers so rapidly that they may appear half-naked and a bluish colour from the appearance of the new feathers under the skin. If there are still eggs or young birds in the nest, moulting adults may abandon them (water-rails, canaries). Several water birds, however, do the opposite: swans, geese and some penguins come together, adults and young, to form moulting parties; they are fat, temporarily flightless, feed little, and seek secluded sites where annually, for hundreds of years during this vulnerable period, they have been more or less safe from serious predation.

Some sea birds (puffins, sea-ducks) which live principally by swimming and diving can afford to drop their quill feathers quickly and become flightless for a week or two until their new plumage is grown. But in storm petrels, which live most of their lives on the wing, exposed to wind and wave, it is essential to retain effective wing-power as well as a thick waterproof coat to keep the body warm and dry. The wing moult therefore is necessarily a long-drawn-out process—feather by feather; 'the eleven primaries are moulted descendently' (Scott, 1970). This adult moult may even begin towards the end of the incubation period: one quill in the left

Canada geese moulting

wing, and its counterpart in the right wing, fall out; twelve tail quills are likewise moulted 'centrifugally in pairs', starting while still feeding the young. The replacements are well sprouted, if not quite full grown, before the next pair is moulted. The wings and tail thus remain intact and powerful enough to carry our petrel thousands of kilometres south. The annual moult of all the worn and faded body feathers continues slowly in the summer days and nights of winter quarters—so slowly that some adults on arrival back at the breeding grounds may still be in partial moult. But some of these may be young adults, which begin their moult later in the winter, have never bred before, and may not do so that summer. Fledgeling storm petrels do not moult until about nine months old.

Flight Speed

Does that 'innate fury' to migrate which, as already described, impels the night warbler and many other migrants (cuckoo, swallow, Arctic tern) to beat their wings for a limited number of hours by night or during the day (depending on whether it is a diurnal or nocturnal traveller), assail our dainty fragile-looking storm petrel, too? Is it not already exhausted by the long days of the southern summer spent in search of food, dancing like a butterfly over the upwelling Benguela and Mozambique currents? It does not seem possible that within three or four months after arrival at the Cape feeding grounds it will have acquired the strength and will to fly, flutter, skim and walk a surface distance of about 14,000km to return to Skokholm and its other breeding islands in late April and May.

We may try to calculate the speed of our little petrel's migration from timing its passage during rare opportunities of observation of individuals moving purposefully past short measured distances of coast. From these occasions we have been able to estimate in round figures a maximum average surface speed of just over 50km (30 miles) per hour. If, during that fury of migration (if it exists in the storm petrel), it maintained that speed for a whole day of twelve hours (and reasonably allowing it the other twelve hours for resting and feeding) then it would cover $50 \times 12 = 600$km a day. In twenty-three days, therefore, it could reach Skokholm; allowing it some further leeway of 25 per cent of this period for contrary winds and other delaying hazards, we arrive at a round figure of one month—which is about the minimum period which, according to the limited dated records of its appearances along the route between Britain and South Africa, our storm petrel takes to accomplish its long journey from the late summer of the Cape Province to the early summer of Europe. Trade winds happen to be more favourable to assist the northward than the southward migration.

On this northern voyage the Cape-wintered adults must cross the equator at the Gulf of Guinea, not improbably pausing to feed on the immature sardine and squid in the tidal currents flowing around the islands of Annobon and Sao Thome (where your plane may refuel during the flight Johannesburg–London). Off Cape Lopez, our petrels may be glad to hasten on northwards, away from days of tropical heat when the fickle Gulf winds are light or variable. The farther they keep to sea the better the lift from the south-east trade wind which blows freshly 500km offshore, away from the Guinea counter-current. North of the Ivory Coast all the way to the Canary Islands in latitude 30°N, the experienced voyagers from the Cape will pass through the wintering ground of their children of last summer. As they have never seen them clearly, and only heard their tremulous infant voices (growing to a plaintive treble piping near fledging time) six months or so earlier, they will not recognise them as such. Even if they did, which I do not believe likely, or even possible, the child will have no urge to follow its parents north. With undeveloped gonads, its sexual appetite will not be aroused for at least another year. Although now in full adult plumage, it is a very young adolescent, still learning how to survive in an abrasive marine world where swift death comes to the unwary, weak and sick. The weaned, independent young bird has its own way to make in life, rich with adventure, and surprises—for the human observer.

Lone First Flight

We left (page 65) the fledgeling storm petrel at the critical moment of its first flight—into the darkness of the autumn night. It seems reasonable to suppose that, like the young shearwater, it must exercise and strengthen its untried wings for an hour or so each night, then return to the safety of the nest, before the actual night of take-off. But we have never been able to observe this, and surely we would have seen it happen when strolling at night to examine our phlegmatic young shearwaters sitting outside their burrows doing just that! However, we know from tests made by releasing fledgeling storm petrels at sea by day, that they are at once capable of flying from the hand, non-stop, for as far as you can follow their dancing erratic flight into the ocean. They seem anxious to escape as fast as they may from the dangers of the land. But what tells them that the land is dangerous, since up to that moment the land has been their sole shelter, home and security?

Autumn is the season of the so-called equinoctial gales—the hour of the greatest mortality in the lives of inexperienced fledgeling oceanic birds. Those which reach the sea for the first time in some Indian-summer calm, as not seldom happens, are fortunate. More often the end of September is windy, with occasional south-westerly gales of up to Force 10. When such storms persist many young birds are 'wrecked' at sea, their bodies devoured by predators or washed ashore. Bird-watchers like to undertake what are known as beach patrols at such seasons—or indeed at any time—gathering information on the species and number of casualties. But many, especially the smaller species such as storm petrels, shearwaters and puffins, are blown far inland, alive and exhausted; so far indeed that the distinguished ornithologist T. A. Coward considered that there was a regular overland autumn migration of shearwaters across England—until it was found that each inland recovery was associated with gales within hours or days beforehand.

The southward autumn passage of our storm petrels is most marked at prominent headlands along western coasts of Britain and north-western Europe, from Cape Wrath and the Butt of Lewis in Scotland, south to Cape Clear (Ireland), Land's End (Cornwall), and Ile d'Ouessant (Brittany). Here also, during the breeding season, you may see feeding movements in any direction of adult and non-breeding flocks and individuals. But much depends on the weather, an inshore wind helping to drift the flying birds closer to these viewpoints. A much slighter but regular southward migration occurs in the North Sea, along the east coast of Britain towards the Straits of Dover; these must be adults and fledgelings from the northern colonies of Orkney, Shetland and probably the Faeroes and Norway. In the English Channel they will be joined by birds breeding or born on small islets off the Channel Islands.

Unless he has a keener eye than we have, or is lucky enough to be close to them when they pass a headland or boat, the watcher will hardly be able to distinguish the fledgeling from the older petrel. The differences between new young and old worn plumage are too indistinct at any distance, unless a gap is noticed in the adult wing where a quill has lately been moulted. For the fledgeling does not begin its first moult until it has settled down in winter quarters. Here its body feathers begin to be shed early in the New Year. The flight feathers will not be shed before the adolescent is nearly a year old in the following June; and by the same gradual process of moulting them in pairs, flying ability is not impaired. The complete moult takes six months.

The first migratory flight of the fledgeling follows approximately for 3,000km that of its parents, the experienced travellers who have gone ahead, eager to reach their far-south winter quarters in the warm summer days off the Cape of Good Hope. On a broad front the southward-flying storm petrels pass the Straits of Gibraltar, Madeira and its off-islets, the Canaries (where some storm petrels have been recorded as nesting), to reach the bulge of western Africa at Cape Verde and the outlying Cape Verde Islands.

As far as banding, observation and collecting records indicate, the under one-year-old storm petrels do not cross the equator, but settle for their first winter in this warm tropical zone where they mingle with other migrants from the north: several species of tern, skuas, gulls and gannets. They may be joined by young storm petrels which have been born on several small islets in the western Mediterranean, from the Adriatic, Corsican, Sicilian, Tunisian and Balearic coasts; but the information on these small colonies and the migrations of adults or young therefrom, past and present, is remarkably scanty. Some of these colonies may have been wiped out recently by the pollution and other effects of human activity in this enclosed sea, which has lately been described by several critics as a lifeless desert.

Behaviour at Sea

Why do our young birds halt short of the equator? Their wings have grown strong during the southward flight, and every feather is firmly in place. Yet they do not press onwards. What are they doing in their winter quarters, that compels them to remain, when their parents are 7,000km farther south? What is the daily routine that makes the tropical climate and seas so attractive? The days and nights in these low latitudes are almost equal in length in which to feed by day and rest by night—if they do rest much at all. Almost certainly they do sleep at intervals when quietly floating on a calm surface. But the more we learn about the flight capabilities of certain birds, the more we are astonished at their apparent endurance. The restless-winged storm petrels in winter quarters north of the equator will have seen, without comprehending, the Arctic terns passing on their world-record migration between Greenland and Antarctica, seemingly forever in flight, never settling on the sea to swim, but getting their fish food by snatching it while hovering close above the waves. I can find no reliable record of this graceful swallow of the sea settled on the water (I have seen it once or twice resting on a floating log of driftwood). Still more remarkable is the winter flight of the common swift *Apus apus*, which during its winter sojourn in Africa has never been seen to go to roost on land. It is certain that the storm petrel can fly for very long periods with ease; it is, however, occasionally seen floating at rest upon the sea.

For lack of regular observation at this age we can only speculate on how immature storm petrels behave in their first winter at sea, from studies of the larger coastal species of sea birds more easily observed in daylight as the fledgelings leave home to get a living on their own. We may try to formulate a pattern to fit the young storm petrel, typical of the survival behaviour of the adolescent migrant.

First of all, the necessity of eating to live produces food-seeking activities derived from natural innate appetite, which informs the bird what is most edible. Having achieved that all-important insurance for survival and health, it has to adapt to other and harsher conditions of oceanic life very different from those of the secure dark warmth and shelter of the nest, where it was so lately fed and cosseted for two months with virtually no problems.

All birds whose parents do not associate with and protect them after weaning must re-learn social behaviour without benefit of parental example. If they are to survive they must learn the hard facts that there are many animals which will actively hunt and kill them. Is fear of enemies largely innate? At this tender moment of fledging probably 10 per cent of young storm petrels are destroyed by predators, and another 10 per cent by autumnal storms. These are round-figure estimates of mortality rates which will leave enough young birds to survive to breeding age. In a stable population the replacement of the old must equal the recruitment to breeding of the younger components.

The fledgeling storm petrels which escaped safely from their natal crevice did so by their greater fitness, arguing a greater awareness, innate or quickly acquired, to get away from the gulls and other diurnal dangers of the land, and be far to sea by daybreak. We have shown how the fat and heavy fledgeling shearwater, which in calm weather is unable to fly on reaching the sea, escapes predators by diving and swimming some distance under water; but we have never seen a storm petrel behave like this. The adult storm petrel makes occasional shallow dives while feeding, but ordinarily, with webbed feet dangling and now and then touching the water, we believe its intention is not to dive; it actively prevents submergence by pushing at or bouncing from the surface with those comparatively large webs.

Another point is that such a small bird is at risk from attack by underwater predators, such as large fish and seals. We have found a number of our shearwaters (which freely dive for fish food) with one leg, or the lower half of one foot, missing—evidently severed by a predatory fish or seal. In the southern hemisphere I have seen sea-lions and leopard seals attack penguins, which can only escape by fast swimming and contortions under water. In the sub-Antarctic the little prions and diving petrels, only a few centimetres larger than our storm petrel, escape in like manner, though many less nimble individuals are likely to be devoured. Bands from some Skokholm shearwaters have been recovered from the stomachs of large fish, for example from an angler-fish weighing 18kg caught off a pier in Brittany on 4 June 1937; although a bottom-dweller, this fish with enormous mouth and formidable teeth does come towards the surface at night.

Learning to be Sociable

Surviving these hazards, by keeping a safe distance away, getting to know its enemies, our fledgeling, if it is to breed successfully when mature, must break down the barrier of individual or 'safety' distance and learn to mix with others of its species. Many animals are solitary by habit and do not begin to associate with a prospective mate until the approach of the breeding season, unless there is the overwhelming attraction of a concentrated food source, as when ravens I have seen in Shetland assemble at waste offal dumps, and bald eagles at the waste outfall from a salmon cannery in British Columbia.

Our fledgeling storm petrel achieves its first socialisation by coming upon a concentrated mass of planktonic and small fish fry at some point along its migration route and while in winter quarters. In the excitement of feeding on a dense ball of this food, the petrels flutter within wing-touching distance, probably uttering cries too faint for the human ear. Usually there will be other species present, making louder cries, attracted to the large fish which will be pursuing the krill and diatoms at the centre; in West African waters in winter there will be pelagic terns, gulls, skuas and gannets, and very likely dolphins. Unfortunately for the last, they and the whirling aerial mass of sea birds attract fishermen using the deadly purse-nets, which will be set out to encircle the shoal, and anything that fails to escape through the meshes or leap to freedom over the line of buoys at the surface is at their mercy.

Where there are such concentrations of sea animals feeding together, our storm petrel avoids too close contact with the large predators; it skims around on the perimeter, picking up morsels of food too small to attract the others. Noticeably too, it will follow fishing boats which are gutting their catch, and while the larger sea birds are greedily competing for the main mass of offal as it slithers through the scuppers, the finer scraps, bits of liver (a special titbit) and lumps of congealed blood are mopped up by storm petrels to the rear of the moving boat.

This common flocking upon a source of food brings that pleasant sensation of filling the stomach. Not enough is known of the hierarchy or peck-order in pelagic flocks, but it is almost certain to be based on seniority and experience—as observed in man, gannets, starlings and many other gregarious species. The juvenile is likely to be at the bottom of this order of precedence in enjoying the best food and living space. The one-year-old petrel will be below the two-year-old, and so on to maturity, to the most vigorous and experienced adult dominant enough to drive away underlings and competitors. Might is generally right in nature's competitive world. However, we really know nothing about the psychological relationships between individuals in the storm-petrel flock at sea, where except when feeding on a concentrated ball of plankton the birds are loosely spaced apart, tirelessly searching the surface to find enough food to refuel that tiny body. Thus spread out, many pairs of eyes cover more potentially food-rich ground. Like vultures scattered across the sky, when the individual discovers food and remains feeding in one spot, the nearest neighbours soon notice, and hasten to share the meal. The flock has its uses, and although we cannot prove it, the coming together for daily meals may engender a form of friendship between individuals, a loose attachment that might last all winter and into the spring.

The sojourn in the warmth of the tropics is for these young birds evidently a time of learning in the great school of the ocean, as well as a holiday among their adolescent peers; generally a pleasant time, we would like to believe, with few serious gales or other hazards. The north-east trade wind is fairly constant, increasing from dawn onwards each day (as we have experienced it on the remote sub-tropical islands of the Desertas and Selvagens), but dying away almost to a calm by night. So pleasant indeed that some juveniles will remain for another year in this tropical routine, making short forays in summer some distance north perhaps. Banding results indicate that none, or very few, reach their northern birthplace until they are two or three years old.

Going Home

When the fledgeling departed from the nest in such a hurry in the dark autumn night, without so to speak a backward glance at the environs of its island home, did it have time to imprint upon the blank memory cells of its developing brain the exact position of the crevice in which it was born? It would of course, during its zigzagging flight away from Skokholm, surely glimpse the dark mass of the island cliffs behind it, even on a night of thick cloud. But, supposing it is true (from the experiments we have mentioned) that birds steer by the stars, if it left the island (and some surely do) on a night of totally obscured sky, how can it remember the way back when, in later years, it is ready to find a mate and breed? As we shall presently relate, some storm petrels do not return to their birthplace island to breed. However, all animals, even those without fixed abodes, must return to breed somewhere if the species is to survive. Marking has proved that the majority do return to the colony in which they were reared, or close to it.

The stimulus to mate is the result of the maturation of the gonads some weeks or months before copulation. But a prerequisite is good health, through having absorbed an adequately rich food supply before the endocrine glands (of internal secretion) are activated to produce hormones and other chemical components which flow through the bloodstream, resulting in ovulation in the female and spermatogenesis in the male. The most important gland for the production of sex hormones is the anterior pituitary at the base of the skull, which appears to be linked with the intrinsic periodicity or seasonal rhythm of the bird's behaviour pattern. Evidently in the storm petrel under one year old, at the time when its parents are already landing again by night in May (at Skokholm), this physiological stimulus is absent or very weak—as it is in very young humans, not yet teenagers. It is a popular theory that photo-periodism—the regulation of the physiological cycle by the amount of daylight available—is the main external stimulus to breeding in birds, especially in those high latitudes where day-length increases more rapidly in the spring than at the equator. But this rule has its exception, already mentioned: the emperor penguin begins to mate when winter darkness is closing down on the frozen Antarctic continent, and it finishes nesting about midsummer, when the sun remains permanently above the polar horizon! There are also several species of large petrels which begin to breed in the autumn.

Our surprising young petrel has not completed its first annual moult, and evidently feels no inclination in May or June to do more than fly a few hundred miles north along the coast, by which mini-migration it will escape the higher temperatures of the low latitude in which it spent its first winter—we can imagine that the midsummer heats and calms of the Cape Verde coast are somewhat stifling. Here, perhaps (allowing us to use our imagination again) it might even explore along the rocky shore and cliffs of the mainland or the many small islands adjacent (Canaries, Desertas), and go ashore, attracted by some other lone juvenile which has already found a dry crevice and is purring an invitation just like a grown-up. There the lone singer, or the pair, may play at housekeeping like any other children. You may think this is too anthropomorphic; yet this is what happens a year or two later. How else are these youngsters to get acquainted, and build up that lasting relationship which will shame many a human couple by its steadfastness?

'Ah, exquisitely formed and beautiful young petrel, how my soul admired you, all the more as I tried to unravel, and you permitted my glimpses into, your wonderful adventurous way of life!

' "Away with you—leave me free!" you seem to say, as I lift you out of the mist-nets we have erected on Priest, the southernmost of the Hebridean Summer Isles. "Why are you burdening me with this leg-ring? I spit on you—there!" ' And spit the little creature did. By the end of two hours of mist-netting several hundred petrels with Tony Mainwood, our clothes were well perfumed with the musky smell of their oil. But all in the good cause of marking petrels, which has brought new knowledge of the movements of *Hydrobates*, and of how long it may live.

After that first winter, followed by a summer in the same oceanic feeding zone north of the equator, the juvenile petrel, barely two years out of the egg, feels a stronger impulse to fly north, but too late to receive guidance from the old birds. By the time it arrives near or at its birthplace its parents are busy incubating. Mist-netting these juveniles suggests that on average, although they fly over established homes occupied by breeding adults, they do not necessarily land. They have simply been attracted by the volume of crooning from below ground, and are reconnoitring, with no great ambition to find and reserve a desirable crevice for future breeding. Round and round they fly, swooping towards the purring voices from the rocks above which our line of nets is erected. Tony and his helpers are ready to rush forward as each excited bird hits the semi-invisible nylon nets. Each one to do so drops softly into the folds between the three or four lengthwise selvedges, unhurt, and awaiting collection. We slip each into a separate linen bag, and take it back to the tent for banding and expert examination (for age—those without bare brood spots are obviously immatures; for parasites, and moult).

The whole mist-netting operation is over in about $2\frac{1}{2}$ hours. There is first the 'fall' of adult petrels into the nets as they arrive from the sea, each going straight to its nest under the boulders to relieve its mate or feed the chick; then a flight in and flitting about of juveniles, which may or may not come to earth, and get caught in the nets; then, long before the first light of the summer dawn, those adults which have been housekeeping below, and some adolescents without eggs, emerge singly at intervals from the burrows. Some are netted, but others, flitting low over the ground, escape.

Recoveries of some of the several thousand storm petrels banded in this way indicate that once they have arrived for the summer—May to

September—the adults are able to gather sufficient food in the sea within about one hundred kilometres of the nest. Late summer is a time of abundant new-hatched small fry in the local seas, small enough for storm petrels to feed upon; as well as of immense surface-swimming shoals of mackerel and herring which share this summer feast and are themselves harvested by the tonne daily by net fishermen. But the younger non-breeding storm petrels do not necessarily return night after night to the same breeding colony. Some may appear in another part of the same island when the mist-nets are tried out there by night. Even more fascinating is the roving habit of some of these two-, three-, and four-year-old adolescents, paying visits in summer to islands and shores scores or hundreds of kilometres away from the place where they were first banded.

A recapture of a banded bird is technically known as a control (ie it has come under control, however briefly, alive or dead). Many of the mist-netted birds are wanderers from other colonies; that is, they were not born on the one where they were first caught and banded. There is a considerable exchange of roaming adolescents, for example, between the storm petrels breeding upon or visiting Fair Isle, halfway between Orkney and Shetland, and Foula Island, a distance of about 80km—say two hours' steady flight.

Skokholm-banded storm petrels have travelled up and down the length of the Irish Sea, south to Brittany, and west to the south of Ireland, being caught most often where observers are out at night on islands where bird observatories operate. Thus in Wales there is an exchange between Skokholm and Bardsey Island (150km), and between Skokholm/Skomer and Copeland (in the North Channel, 330km). Curiously, the storm petrel has not been found breeding on Copeland; one of these Copeland controls had been ringed on Skokholm fifteen days earlier, and was retrapped back on Skokholm two years later in May, when most likely it had settled to nest there—few non-breeders are mist-netted before June. Four other birds banded at Skokholm were recovered at Copeland one, two, three and four years, respectively, after banding (Mainwood, 1976).

Although there may be an undiscovered colony of storm petrels nesting on Copeland, it is clear that during the summer, June to September, numbers are flying at night past this island which lies in the shipping fairway east of Belfast Lough, which must also be a feeding zone for them. It has now become routine among mist-netters to play a tape-recording of the storm petrels' invitatory purring song wherever they suspect storm petrels might be visiting. This has led to some surprising discoveries: for example that these little birds, during the summer season of wandering, will come flying in towards the taped sound at several places on the east coast of Scotland, where they are not known to nest and are hardly ever seen, except during the southward autumn migration which takes place at some distance offshore. Playing a tape of the purring song on the Isle of May, Firth of Forth, produced a response from a hole in the rocks where a pair were found to be nesting—a new record! There was an earlier record (1904) of breeding on the Bass Rock; and it may well be that playing tapes on other small rocky islands of this Firth will reveal hitherto unsuspected breeders.

One quiet July night, walking along the platform of boulder-battered cliffs at Reiff, opposite the Summer Isles in Rosshire, Scotland, we heard numerous squeakings of petrels in the air. Here Tony Mainwood set up his nets one calm August night and caught 106 petrels; all must have been non-breeders. One had been banded the previous year in Orkney, over 160km by sea. Ten were recaptured in the next summer in mist-nets set above the huge colony in the rocks of Priest, one of the uninhabited Summer Isles. (Priest has since become a sanctuary for these petrels and for greylag geese, otters and other fauna, under the Royal Society for the Protection of Birds, largely we believe as the result of the intensive study and marking of many thousands of storm petrels there by Tony Mainwood.) Mist-netting on Priest Island over ten years has paid dividends in the rising number or ratio of retraps (controls) to new birds caught, using the nets each summer in the same positions in the 'Valley of the Petrels' as we called it when camping with Tony; the results show that up to one-third are controls.

Catching birds in this way, without harming them, has always been a great excitement for me, appealing to both the hunting instinct and scientific curiosity, with special reward when you find in your hand a bird banded earlier, and perhaps far away. But you must be patient before you can obtain the details of where and when it was banded, after you have forwarded to the banding headquarters your recovery data and the all-important number and inscription on the leg-ring; the 'control' may even be a bird banded overseas by a foreign observer. A group of banders including Tony Mainwood has lately visited the large nesting colonies of both storm and Leach's fork-tailed petrels in the Faeroe Islands, with valuable results—proving an interchange between these and the northern Scottish colonies.

From all these records and controls we now have a clearer picture of the typical behaviour of the young petrel. After two years of living in sub-tropical seas off West Africa, our Mother Carey's Chicken makes its first approach to the place where it was born, but will not normally land until it is three years old—in the third summer of its life. It may travel north along western coasts within several hundred kilometres, where there is adequate summer feeding. A minority will become attached to some other colony within this wide range of its ocean territory, where it enjoys plentiful summer feed; and, what is important for the future, it makes closer acquaintance with potential mates.

Banding large numbers of fledgeling petrels is a much less simple task.

Born in inaccessible crevices they are hard to reach, but may be mist-netted as they emerge at midnight in late September and October, when they can be identified by the fresh appearance of the unmoulted plumage ('lead bloom' it has been called) and no vestige of a brood patch. From the few hundred which have been banded and subsequently controlled, we know that some begin to look for permanent homes by entering crevices and holes in their fourth summer, although usually too late to breed. But they form a first partnership in this way, by common adoption of a site. They will indulge in courtship, breaking the barrier of individual distance. They will meet again earlier in the next summer when five years old; and a suitable safe nesting site being available, the hen will lay a fertile egg for the first time. Each year thereafter they will meet at the well-remembered nest site—at Skokholm as early as late April, but usually in May; and the breeding cycle already described in earlier chapters is established.

The experienced breeders know their homes, and stick to them. But of course there are casualties and natural deaths in any adult population, and the bereaved partner must seek a new one; banding indicates that this is what has happened when the established bird is found mated to a new unringed partner—most likely from the pool of four- to six-year-old bachelors or maidens. Divorce is so rare that if a pair fail to arrive together in the spring, one suspects that some accident has occurred to one of them. An early nesting failure, resulting in loss of the egg has, however, been recorded as resulting in subsequent loss of interest in each other. Such failed breeders are believed to account for the proportion of mature birds which are caught away from their established colony; they have become wing-loose and fancy-free for the rest of the summer.

Longevity

How long may a bird as small as a storm petrel live? As yet we do not know more than that the oldest-known British storm petrel—as far as we have been able to trace in the banding literature—is an individual which was marked as full-grown in 1950, and was last seen alive in 1969. It had lived twenty years at least, allowing a minimum of two years before returning to land, if it was immature when first ringed. (The oldest-known Leach's petrel has lived twenty-four years—see next chapter.)

It is tempting to indulge in some simple calculations, by taking the age of five years (average) for first laying of an egg; the fact that only one egg is laid annually to each fertile female and her mate; and the known average annual survival rate of banded birds returning to burrows under observation; and trying to arrive at longevity figures, as well as the age composition of a normal colony of storm petrels of a known constant population. According to Scott (1970), the annual survival rate of adults at Skokholm is 87–88 per cent; we could perhaps make that a round figure of 90 per cent, to allow for some human-observer interference which is known to cause a degree of desertion of marked nest sites. As the sex ratio appears to be equal in all populations studied, the storm petrel must enjoy a life-expectancy close to that of other animals, such as seals, dolphins, gannets, gulls and many other sea birds, which breed at this slow rate: that is, first successful reproduction at five years, and thereafter a single chick annually. In the Skokholm petrel, Scott found in his marked burrows that hatching success (214 eggs laid) averaged 62 per cent, 'the most important single cause of failure being infertility'. But less than 50 per cent of eggs laid resulted in young fledged.

We supposed that a pictorially attractive life-expectancy graph might be drawn up from these and other published figures, but the experienced statisticians of the mathematical faculty at Auckland University made an attempt (which we acknowledge with thanks here), and were dissatisfied that such data could be used for a reliable calculation of age composition and longevity. There are too many variables—such as assuming that the juvenile and adult survival rate are the same, which is hardly likely in view of migration of the inexperienced youngsters dawdling in the tropics, while the older birds fly rapidly to winter, or summer, quarters through low latitudes. After working out a formula from the above data, Professor George Seber summarises: 'Assuming a constant survival rate of about 90 per cent for all ages, including juveniles, and assuming a stationary population, then about 47 per cent of the population would be juveniles (ages one to five inclusive). If this makes sense, it is probably worth quoting; otherwise the calculation is best ignored.'

At a guesstimate, the proportion of such juveniles to adults does seem somewhere near parity, from our experience and that of others in observing and banding British storm petrels at mist-nets when the nightly midsummer (July) 'fall' of incoming birds fly in above the breeding colony. Furness & Baillie (1981) mist-netted 1,490 storm petrels on St Kilda in 1978, and another 909 in 1980, but could make no satisfactory conclusion statistically as to age composition. Again there were too many variables, including differences when taped calls were used to lure, and no tapes were used; nor were state of brood patch, or of body weight, consistent. They considered the use of standardised 'catch rates', but conclude that 'Catch rate is highly dependent on wind speed but not apparently greatly influenced by other weather factors. Differences in catch rates may provide a useful measure of nonbreeder activity and the relative densities of different breeding colonies.'

8
Leach's fork-tailed storm petrel

One calm moonlit night at Skokholm fifty years ago, watching and listening as we rested amid the jumble of boulders and red sandstone screes under the western headland, we heard a strange cry above the murmur of hundreds of storm petrels flitting around us and in their crevices in the rocks. I had first discovered this largest colony of these little birds on the island when chipping the slaty rock in the summer of 1928, trying in my amateurish way to shape new stone tiles from the vein of yellowish sandstone which is exposed here, the site of a quarry which produced these heavy tiles to roof the island buildings a few centuries ago. Marks of those early rock masons were still plain in the chiselled strata; we needed to fashion a few score new tiles to repair those roofs.

A loud, almost quacking note from the air, quite different from the familiar cry of the storm petrel, yet impossible to put into onomatopoeic words—as I tried at the time, and as other listeners have since found; some modern bird-identification books now insert tape-recorded sonograms. It was also impossible to see it clearly in the aerial maze of the smaller petrels. Only when I got back to the house and searched *The Practical Handbook of British Birds* did I realise that the solitary loud-singing visitor in that purring crowd must have been Leach's fork-tailed petrel *Oceanodroma leucorhoa*. I was never to see or hear it again at Skokholm, but subsequently, during extensive mist-netting in later years by other observers at Skokholm, a single Leach's has been caught at rare intervals. Its nearest known British breeding sites at that time were about 400 surface kilometres away as the bird would fly around the south-west of Ireland to the Blasket Isles off Kerry. Even so, none had been found breeding there since 1899; there was mention of tiny islets named Tearaght and Inish-na-bro where a few Leach's petrels were discovered in the last century incubating their single egg. Still, it was exciting to think that this rare British bird might perhaps be nesting on some of the more remote islands strung along the southern coast of Ireland, which might explain the occasional visit of an individual to Skokholm. At least it provided me with one of several excuses to go and look for it in the Blasket Islands. Apart from my natural passion for small islands,

I had lately read that masterpiece of island autobiography, *Twenty Years Agrowing* by Maurice O'Sullivan.

August 1937 began with a heat wave; and another wave—of visitors on holiday. Ever since we had started the first British bird observatory on Skokholm, with that object in view, amateur naturalists had come to help in the work of banding both resident sea birds and migrant land birds. Mist-nets had not yet been introduced, but we had several fixed and portable wire-netted traps and enclosures excellent for capturing birds. Early in the autumn, from the end of July onwards, numbers of small woodland and moorland birds passed through the island, many coaxed into the traps by providing food, water and cover. Catching, banding and releasing these was a special joy—you never knew what species might turn up; some, thought to be rare visitors to this coast, have proved to be regular passage migrants.

The experiments, referred to earlier, on testing the homing ability of sea birds, were well under way; the first of two shearwaters sent by air to Venice and released there on 9 July, was sitting complacently with its mate in their burrow close behind the island cottage, when we lifted the lid above this marked nest on the evening of 24 July. I noted in my diary: 'A wonderful feat, the more remarkable because it has come in on a night of brilliant moonlight, which shearwaters do not always like to do. In the fortnight it has been away its mate has hatched the egg, and tonight presented its partner with a lively downy chick! I wonder what the traveller had to say to the faithful housekeeper? How clever of it to find its way so quickly!'

By air Venice is 930 miles in a straight line, but by sea (and shearwaters never seem to fly over the land willingly) the distance, via the Adriatic and Strait of Gibraltar, is 3,700 miles. The British Consul in Venice, who had

Leach's storm petrel at entrance to burrow

released the shearwaters, wrote that one bird flew in a southerly direction towards the open sea, but the other wheeled inland westward towards the high Appenine mountains—in the overland direction of Skokholm! Either way she could hardly have had time for random searching for the correct heading for Skokholm. She instinctively 'knew' the way, though our shearwater does not ever penetrate the Adriatic; and moreover, since she was plump and glossy, she had fed herself well at sea, ready to resume incubation—but her mate had completed that task. Yes, the island at this time was a stimulating place to be; and now, with thoughts of a holiday ourselves, my wife and I accepted the offer of Morrey Salmon, distinguished Cardiff naturalist, and his wife, to supervise the observatory work and its enthusiastic volunteers. At last we could go in search of those fork-tailed petrels in far south-west Ireland—a new land to us.

But first, why should not Leach's fork-tailed petrel nest on the little island of Grassholm, away to the west of Skokholm? We had several times visited this rocky, grassy hump of 22 acres, about seven miles across the Wild Goose tide-race of St Géorge's Channel. Waterless in summer, it was yet once, long ago, evidently during the Viking raids on this coast—all the islands have Viking names—temporarily inhabited, from the evidence of remains of stone-walled huts and enclosures, now just heaps of stones ideal for small nesting petrels.

On 1 August, more than a dozen of us embarked for Grassholm in perfect weather. During three hours' intensive search of likely crevices in the tumbled stones and among the peaty ruins of the great puffinry (which once contained by estimation half a million puffins—in 1890) we could find no sign or smell of any storm petrels. Not that sniffing after them with nose to crevices was much good on this island where 5,000 pairs of gannets were nesting, and the strong whiff of their fishy city filled your nostrils. But three years earlier we had camped for a week on the island making the film *The Private Life of the Gannets* (it won an Oscar at Hollywood subsequently) with Julian Huxley, and each night had listened in vain for the familiar purring petrel song.

There are Welsh legends which tell of Grassholm as a place of banishment or sojourn, associated with the Celtic invasion of Ireland from Wales in pre-Christian times. The Welsh book of legends of eleventh-century origin, the *Mabinogion*, describes 'a fair royal palace with a great hall in Gwales in Penfro (Grassholm in Pembrokeshire) where people passed fourscore years so that they were not aware of having ever spent a time more joyous and serene than that'. You get that feeling of timelessness on this wondrous bird-haunted Viking-named holm. But in fact the stone huts and one large enclosure were more likely the work of visiting bird-fowlers (an art much practised in Viking Norway, Ireland and the Faeroes), harvesting the

Gannet breeding colony

gannets and puffins each autumn at fledging time. Our party that August day was satisfied with banding over 800 young gannets—part of the observatory's continuing study each summer, when weather permitted a landing on this harbourless islet.

Cape Clear to the Blasket—for Forky-tails

There is an overnight ferry from Fishguard to Cork in the south of Ireland. A few days later my wife and I were speeding by the Bantry Bay bus over rutted lanes, punctuated with long pauses at village inns to discharge and load ever-cheerful southern Irish passengers and their families, all dressed in their Sunday best—for it was Sunday, a day of rest and enjoyment once you had been to Mass. At last the beautiful outlines of the Caha Mountains swam into view. At four in the afternoon we were unloaded in Bantry town itself. We were unsure how we would reach the outer islands, but as luck would have it we were given a lift over the hills to Roaringwater Bay. The sun was low over the sea. We were about to book a room at Schull, that snug haven beloved of sailing men, when we fell in with a merry crew of four fishermen and two colleens. 'The best way to Cape Clear Island? Yerra, now wouldn't that be strange, and we ourselves from the Cape! Well, now, come aboard and welcome, man and woman of Wales.' For so we had explained ourselves in telling of our wish to set foot on the most south-western island of the British Isles.

Thirty feet long, decked forward, the *Inishclear* had mainsail, spinnaker and jib, and without an engine she needed every inch of canvas to beat against the summer wind seven miles to the north haven of Cape Clear Island. All the crew and colleens had taken off their shoes and stockings before boarding their clean-looking craft, but we were excused with a laughing 'Not at all, not at all'. The reason for barefootedness was apparent when, with the sail steadying the little ship, the girls were soon attempting to dance, as they sang Irish songs. The *Inishclear* made short tacks between Long Island and Castle Island to gain the open bay, moving with a sweet gentle sighing ease over the sheltered water.

In the open sea as night fell, the swift bat-winged forms of storm petrels danced about us; the little waves riding the faint ocean swell were luminescent with swarming plankton and tiny fishes on which they fed. '*Father* Carey's Birds' they were, insisted the young man they called Padruig; though he couldn't be bothered to explain why. He, the girls, all of them, seemed in a dream of joy at the end of their day ashore at Schull. They sang and chattered, and chattered and sang, subsiding sleepily into the refrain 'Rolling home, rolling home to dear old Cape Clear!' in time with the swaying of the boat.

It was so dark we could no longer see the storm petrels except as dim shapes, and imagine we heard their faint cries, straining—a little drowsily it must be admitted, for we had had a long day—for that different note of Leach's fork-tailed. So dark indeed that we were surprised when the great walls of rock enclosing the entrance to Clear harbour loomed up, and by a neat tack the *Inishclear* glided through with enough way, her mainsail dead in the eye of the warm offshore breeze, to tie up to the quay. Away up the road from the sea the lights of the Central Inn were gleaming a welcome, and there came to us first the sounds of violin music, then the light tapping of bare feet on the hard earthen floor—and more song and chatter in the pure Erse, which is the spoken tongue on this remote island. 'God and Mary be with you,' was the greeting of innkeeper Con Regan; and he ordered food and a bed in a separate room to be prepared for the couple from Wales. The melodeon, fiddle, and dance went on and on, putting us quickly to sleep.

All next day we explored this beautiful island of some fifty little farms inhabited by a fine race of upstanding fishermen. Their wives perform most of the land work, tending one or two milch cows, a donkey, goats; and in the shelter of walls of stone heaped from the rocky fields, many as small as gardens, crops of potatoes, oats, seed hay, cabbages, and wheat (for bread). At that time, over forty years ago, they were a nobly independent island people, using hand tools on the land, while few had motors in their boats used to fish for lobsters, crabs and crayfish. Yet everyone we met had all the time in the world to talk with us, and offer the hospitality of their humble stone-built, thatched cottage home. The island priest, seeing us studying choughs soaring over the old Napoleonic tower, and no doubt curious about the visitors from Wales, said: 'If it's birds thee want, then Tim West-End is the bhoy for thee. He knows every feather there is on Cape Clear, and he can speak English.'

Tim became our shadow, and glad we were of his eager expertise and innocent charm. Born in Cork, he was an adopted child, and had the sharpness of the city child combined with a knowledge of birds and beasts gained by living on Clear. His home was a low two-roomed thatched cottage, with walls whitewashed inside and out. Himself and Herself (as his guardians referred to themselves in front of us) had almost no English, but smiled and nodded cheerfully at all we said, whether Tim translated or not. He told us that they had no money, but lived on their own produce and what they might barter for it. Himself at sixty was a good lone fisherman who never came home without a full basket; if it was too rough to fish he would bring back a creel of seaweed for manure, or peat for the hearth—where the fire smouldered all day and night. Herself tended two cows, an ass and poultry, in ten acres divided into as many fields by those stone hedges. They had six sheep running on the common land, providing wool for their homespun clothes.

Tim was a little puzzled by the picture of Leach's petrel in our pocket bird-guide, but thought he could find one in the cliffs if we went there in the late evening, for it was a grand place for the stormies or Father Carey's Chickens. And more than once he inveigled us to stay for the midday meal in the cottage, so that he could talk of the wonders of the bird world, and how he himself was planning to become an 'orthonologist' and see the world. Tranquilly Herself prepared the food as we talked with Tim, sitting on a bench in the living room, furnished with pleasing economy. The bench, a dresser, a low chair, a table, a spinning wheel, a shrine with a candle on the wall, and sack-cushions each side of a hearth furnished with cooking-pot, kettle and frypan; that's all, save for a side of bacon and some fishing gear seen dimly in the rafters. The meal consisted of potatoes boiled in the cooking pot; this was drained of water and the potatoes dried off to a mealy consistency, then emptied piping hot on a clean linen table cloth. You washed your hands, and ate without more ado—or tools or plate. This was their usual midday sustenance; for the evening meal there would be an egg or some fish, and bread made of their own ground wheat, sometimes flavoured with a little bartered maize meal, fresh-cooked in the big iron pot, the lid of which was covered with glowing peat. Tea and sugar were luxuries, for special occasions. On this simple, healthy diet, Himself and Herself at sixty years were the most serene and devoted pair you could imagine. But Tim was as restless as an inquisitive sparrow, sharp-eyed to point out every bird. While my wife collected and listed wild flowers, and sketched and painted the island's beauty (two holiday joys for her), Tim and I rambled the cliffs and wilder places, peering into boggy ravines. He had some appropriate names for the island birds: lady-dish-wash was the pied wagtail; the heron he knew as Judy-the-bogs. He had a little white dog he called Gannets, an undersized sheepdog mongrel with the long legs of a lurcher, which 'told' him the birds; that is, it pointed at birds in cover when it scented them. It might be wild duck, corncrake or pipit, as we pushed through long grass and low scrub on the gorsy slopes, and blackthorn and blackberry thickets. One day, taking shelter in a roofless chapel, we found a robin's late nest in a human skull tumbled from a stone grave.

Heron

Twice we hunted the farthest western headland of the Cape as the sun went down and the light was lit upon the Fastnet Rock a mile or two away in the tide-race. When my torch gave out Tim produced some candles with which we continued the search of the dangerous screes over which numerous petrels were flighting home when dusk had quite fallen. Tim darted hither and thither, not heeding my 'be careful' groans. He kept bringing me adult storm petrels so that I could leg-band them, and begged me to look into this burrow and that crevice, for he thought that the chicks in some of them were . . . 'Bejabers, so huge they must be forky-tails.'

When the inflighting of the little petrels had ceased, we rested awhile on the extreme point of the Cape, and watched the lights of a great transocean liner steaming westwards at 25 knots beyond the Fastnet lighthouse. She swiftly overhauled a trawler which was making a short cut between the island and the Fastnet Rock. It was very beautiful and peaceful in the rare calm of that August midnight; but Tim let loose a flood of talk, including his longing to be a 'sea-naturalist', to be first a fisherman here in Cape Clear, for that way 'Yerra, I want to go to the very end of the seas of all the world!' Adding firmly, as the great liner dwindled in the west on its way to America, 'That way, bejabers I must go, if I'm to see the wonderful wandering albatross thee told me about, the one that takes two years to nest.'

In the cliffs below us petrels were still purring at intervals; if any were Leach's 'forky-tails' they were quite safe and inaccessible there. One whole day was spent around the island coast, and in the same evening we joined a cheerful party of islanders to fish for the giant pollack, known as blackfish, around the Fastnet Rock. As it happened the annual Cowes–Fastnet yacht race was in progress, and before dusk fell we took pictures of the German entry *Aktur* gliding in a smooth sea around the pillar of the lighthouse, shadowed by wheeling fulmar petrels and diving gannets. After sunset, my diary records: 'Little bunches of storm petrels appeared, the most I have ever seen on the sea together. They were feeding, it seems, on planktonic tiny fish, the prey of shoals of sprats and probably mackerel. We caught on our lines many large blackfish, up to three feet long, which rise towards the surface to feed at night. It was soon too dark to identify the species of storm petrels, but they all seemed to be our little *Hydrobates*.'

It was a happy life on Clear Island. Next day we sailed in an island smack to take part in the regatta at Schull: 'The quay at Schull packed with people, provender stalls, cheapjacks, gaming shows, a brass band in uniform. We lazed about, sketching and writing, laughing at the greasy-pole tumbles. Our smack, with usual rig of mainsail, topsail, spinnaker and jib, won one of the sailing races. Once more we returned home in the dusk, convoyed by storm petrels, and the colleens and bhoys singing "Rolling home to Cape Clear".'

Fisherman Mahony at that time had the largest and most reliable motor-boat on Cape Clear Island, and agreed to take us seventy miles north along the coast to the Blasket Islands, in our continuing search for the elusive Leach's fork-tail. It was agreed we should land at any small islets en route, such as the Bull and the Cow, off Dursey Island, weather permitting.

On to the Blaskets

The *Dun Claire* left Clear harbour at 8 a.m., with backward glances at the beautiful island and new friends bidding us farewell from the quay. A flat calm presently changed to a fresh south-west wind, swell and rain, and made landing on the Bull and Cow that day impossible. Mahony headed for the

Choughs

shelter of Castletown Berehaven, came to anchor at 3 p.m., made tea on the ship's tiny coal stove, and fed us large slices of bread and jam. My diary records that it was too stuffy to sleep that night in the tiny cabin of the *Dun Claire*, with the hospitable Mahony and his son; so 'We went for a long stroll in the wild byways east of the port before coming to drink sherry and sleep at the Commercial Inn, nicely old-fashioned and unhurried.'

Next morning (14 August): 'There was a fresh NNW wind, but quiet water as far as Dursey Sound, in which, finding a heavy sea at its north entrance, Mahony turned back and landed us on Dursey Island quay for an hour or two. We strolled up the long road of this delightful, sparsely inhabited island, watching large flights of choughs, thirty in the air together; the red-billed crow seems plentiful along this coast. At 15.00 hours it had calmed enough for us to emerge into the open sea and head for the Bull Rock, a remarkable affair with a cave clean through its base. There was a heavy swell after the night's gale, and it was rather a difficult business to photograph and count the gannet colony. At the cost of being very sick I did so, and estimated there were 400 gannet nests on the Bull.' We headed for the Skellig Rocks, and here on Little Skellig was an immense gannetry; we estimated about 12,000 nests, covering most of this pinnacled rock. But the swell made it too difficult to land; nor could we get near the lighthouse landing steps on Great or Skellig Michael, which we had hoped to do, and see this stone shrine and cell of the Celtic saint.

Mahony hesitated to strike north across the open sea on the long leg to the Blaskets, and for a while steered towards Valentia Island. But he could see we were longing to reach the whaleback hump of Great Blasket with its enticing satellite islets stretching from the Foze Rocks eastwards to the Dingle peninsula. The heavy swell eased as we crossed the wide Dingle Bay. Dusk and storm petrels closed around us as we entered Blasket Sound. The tiny landing place of Great Blasket was deserted. Mahony shouted in Irish: 'Naomhog! Bring out a currach!' Rectangles of yellow light appeared where doors opened on the hillside, dogs barked, black forms appeared on the edge of the low cliffs. Presently a dark shape bobbed over the water towards us—a naomhog or currach (lath-and-canvas canoe) 25ft long and barely 4ft wide. A long discussion in Irish followed between Mahony and a tall Blasket man, one of four in the canoe.

'God and Mary save thee, are ye from the south with a doctor on board, or is it the priest ye have this time o' night?'

'It is from the south we are, from east o' the Fastnet, if ever a Blasket man put his nose south'ard of Valentia! It is no priest or doctor, but a plain man and his wife from Wales we do have, hungry for food, fire and bed.'

From the darkness came the hoped-for reply: 'Bring them into the canoe. We have plenty and welcome. Will ye anchor here?' But Mahony had no trust in the tide-rips of the Blasket anchorage. He hoisted his lights and sailed away south, meaning to take a big slice out of the seventy-mile cruise home before dawn. With the same delightful hospitality as at Clear Island, we were welcomed into the humble stone-and-thatch homes of Blasket— there is no inn here. We were assigned to one, where our seventy-three-year-old hostess had no English, but quickly had the kettle singing over the peat fire, so that it outshrilled the song of the crickets which live on the hearths of these island dwellings.

By chance we had arrived on the eve of a grand event in the island's history—the honouring of a Blasket woman. Many indeed believed we had come specially for this crowning of Peg Sayers with laurels, won for the best literary work in Irish—the Douglas Hyde Award, value £50. It soon got about that I had come from Wales, and the priest invited me to say a few words in Welsh; though, as I cannot read Irish, Peg Sayers' work was unknown to me. But it was a good chance to meet some of the characters described in that other Blasket book, *Twenty Years Agrowing*—in particular Padrig O'Dala, born in those little off-islets where Leach's petrel was supposed to breed. Would he take us there? He would, for he regularly fished for lobster and crayfish around the island of Inishvickillaun, where he had been born. Ah, aye, the island swarmed with stormy petrels.

'What a character is Pat Daly (his English name)!' I wrote in my diary. 'He is a fisherman, and owns Inishvickillaun, builds fiddles (violins) in his spare time. Most of his family have migrated to America, like so many Irish today. "And soon none will be left to man the currachs," said he, when we stepped ashore next day on the tiny beach under the cliffs of his island. "But a man will have better peace here in this inish, where my mother brought me into the world." '

It just shows you what happens if you give your heart to so lonely and lovely a place. You were obliged to admire this fine cove in which we had landed, island wrens singing from the tumbled boulders, sea-beet and ferns hanging from the ledges. A steep winding path led past turf-diggings to the centre of the island, to the homestead built in the shelter of a wild castle of lichened rocks. This was a grey stone building of two rooms separated by a stone partition, but communicating inside—in many ways an island home such as I had first found at Skokholm. It had a sound waterproof Blasket roof of tarred felt; and all around grass in plenty in little stone-walled fields lively with sheep and rabbits. From the doorway leapt Lass the sheep-bitch, left in charge of Pat's flock, trusted to kill nothing but rabbits for her living while her master might be absent. Poor lonely Lass, her real hunger was for companionship. She never left our heels as long as we trod the island.

Away to the west, above the Hollow of the Eagles, lay the Tearaght, a camel-hump of a rock with a lighthouse and three keepers. That evening, over the turf fire, Pat had much to tell about the Tearaght, which I have no space to repeat here. As for the 'forky-tailed stormies' he thought he could find some. Meanwhile he proudly showed me his garden, a stone-hedged enclosure with a bank tall with lobster-pot willow wands, nasturtiums rioting in and out through every hole in the wall. Potatoes looked well, set, as is the custom here, in ridges 2ft across, three rows in each.

Diving his hand under a big stone, Pat pulled out a young storm petrel, then another, both—it seemed to me—identical with our small petrel chicks at home. 'These', said he, 'are Mother Carey's Chickens. Many a time we sought them when we were children in the Inish. My soul, I remember the day my grandfather kept a beautiful garden here! Let me tell you he farmed the Inish a thousand times better than they do be farming the Blasket today.' His son by now had worked up a great turf fire and had a big loaf ready for baking. It was made of three parts white to one of maize flour, with some soda, the dough filling the cooking pot three inches deep. The heavy iron lid was piled high with embers. In an hour a huge yellow loaf was turned out to make room for a mess of roast pollack and wrasse (caught in the trammel net in the bay below), bacon and a big potato each.

'It's many a night,' said Daly, when we had pushed our empty plates on one side and his pipe had been started with an ember from the fire, 'that my grandfather's canoe was loaded to the tacks [holding the canvas of the currach to the wooden gunwale] with mackerel, and not half the net drawn. There's many a boat was sunk with the gifts of the sea. My sorrow, those times do be never seen today.' Rising and peering through the door, he added: 'Tis a fine night, my soul, an' the moon weak yet. We should have good luck by the sheen on the water.' It was very still when we launched the currach, save for scattered shoals of mackerel breaching the surface, their silver faces and huge eyes gleaming in moonlight with a glint of the luminescence from the summer plankton which fills the inshore seas at this time. At the edge of the current rippling through Inish-na-bro Sound, the white rumps of many storm petrels danced around the currach, as they swayed and dipped, feeding with dangling feet touching the now silver-black, now sparkling, surface. Fairy forms too quick to identify, and elfin voices quite drowned by the murmur of the running tide. The net had hardly been laid out to intercept the mackerel than the dark heads of two seals rose at the far end. We caught nothing.

Once more the currach was hauled ashore. The islandmen laid down to sleep by the smouldering peat fire. We wandered around the stone hedge-walls of the former O'Dala farm, as if we had been at Skokholm. There were hundreds of storm petrels flying over the heaped-up stones, so laboriously gathered over centuries of island living. Some were entering or leaving crevices in which young petrels squeaked for food. But more seemed to be just hovering and swooping around; the immatures or virgins which were familiarising themselves with future sites and mates for the serious business of procreation in the next or succeeding years. There is an oratory or tiny stone-built chapel of some monkish recluse of the Celtic church, more than a thousand years old, now the home of the storm petrels. We listened long here for a sound of Leach's petrel, until all was silent in the slow dawn.

A currach came to take us to Inish-na-bro, a long ridged island where this petrel had been found breeding late last century. We fossicked about some half-buried dwellings, raised hut circles and faint outlines of little gardens and fields, now the playground of rabbits, but found no signs of little petrels, though plenty of fulmars had young in the steeper cliffs. Another day we were rowed in one of these banana-shaped currachs, which have fixed oars, and are beautifully managed by Blasket men (no sails are carried), to the northern islet of Inishtooskert. 'Here,' said Kerne, as we walked up to an ancient beehive-shaped stone house, 'was my people born. They lived in this house with children and kine.' His son Tomás lit a fire in the centre of the floor, and soon the acrid smoke from burning heather twigs drove us out of the dark place. As on Inishvickillaun, there is a low roofless chapel, but not in such good repair. There are graves too. Kerne lifted some stones near a moss-grown white quartz stone cross, revealing some yellow leg-bones and part of a human skull. All this, and some other stone-roofed low buildings were part of St Brendan's Oratory, latterly used when the island was farmed by Kerne's grandparents, he said. But only a young wheatear fluttered from the crevice exposed by the opened grave. We stood in the sunlight, wondering when that skull had been filled with a living brain.

A mug of tea, and then Kerne's principal reason for visiting his birthplace was made plain—we saw the Blasket men rounding up sheep and 'rooing' (pulling, not clipping) the ripe fleeces from the island flock.

We worked along the steep western slopes full of holes in the rough grazed turf. Burrow after burrow yielded only a storm-petrel chick to our probing arm and little crooked wire; or, rarely, a single non-breeding adult with no bare brood-spot. Robins, already arrived from mainland haunts, had set up territories here and there, amid stony terraces where once the hermit St Brendan must have heard their plaintive song in the long winter days of his voluntary exile.

Leach's at Last

It was on a visit to another early retreat of the Celtic monks, the Westmann Islands, a few miles south of Iceland, that I held a Leach's fork-tailed storm petrel in my hand for the first time. There I joined fishermen on a cod-lining trip to the string of rocky islands away to the south-west of the main island of Heimay, with Viking names: Alfsey, Brandur, Geldunger, Hellisey, Suderey. Islets which are relics of the still active volcanoes of Iceland; at that moment they were mostly sheer pinnacles of cliffs white with nesting gannets and fulmar petrels. Alfsey and Brandur were green with grass in the remains of their craters, but occupied by thousands of puffins, fulmars and pairs of glaucous gulls; here too pairs of snow-buntings were nesting, and eider ducks along the landing place. I could find no storm petrels at all.

We steered towards Suderey, which seemed to float like a green inverted cauldron in the current. Where a grassy shelf came near the sea's edge one of the fishermen and I leaped ashore. 'Suderey—many stormswala, I show you,' he said eagerly, springing up the steep green slope well ahead of me. About 150 metres up he began tearing at the turf riddled with many small holes. In a few minutes he pulled forth that elusive bird I had sought for so long—a Leach's petrel!

After those years of longing to handle one I was in no hurry to release it. The beautiful black beady eye in the brown-black head looked at me intelligently, I thought, rather than with fear. How innocent of man it really was! How many storms had that eye witnessed? How far over the ocean had those wings flown and these webbed feet pattered? I spread the forked tail, and examined the extent of the white on the rump and wing-fringes. Its life-history, at that moment unknown, must surely be much like that of our Skokholm petrels.

The wind was freshening. No, said the fisherman, I could not be left here. It might be weeks before I could be rescued, it was rare to have a day like this, calm enough to land for a few minutes. Perhaps later, when the

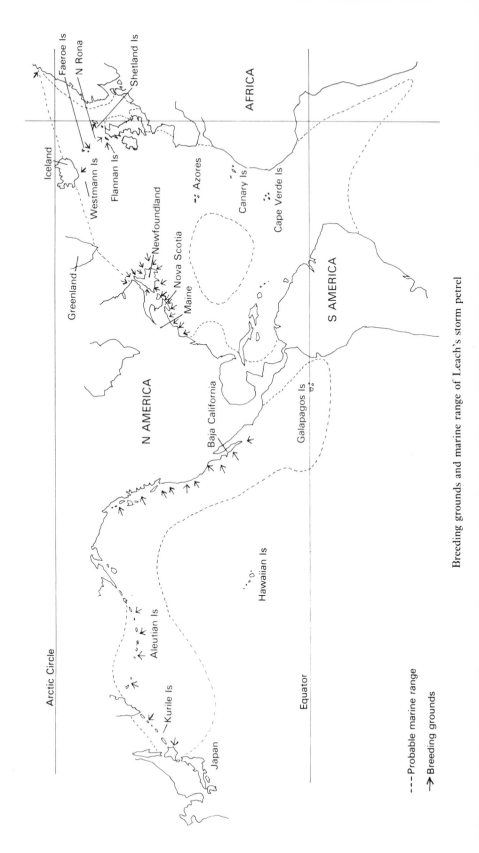

Breeding grounds and marine range of Leach's storm petrel

- - - Probable marine range

→ Breeding grounds

Arctic Circle

AFRICA

Faeroe Is
N Rona
Shetland Is
Iceland
Westmann Is
Flannan Is
Azores
Canary Is
Cape Verde Is

Greenland
Newfoundland
Nova Scotia
Maine

N AMERICA

S AMERICA

Baja California

Galapagos Is

Hawaiian Is

Aleutian Is

Equator

Kurile Is

Japan

Westmann bird-fowlers came to harvest the puffins and fulmar when the young were ready to fly in September, I could camp awhile with them? I let the bird go at last. As its home had been destroyed, I threw it towards the sea. It flew in short darting curves downwards, and was quickly lost in the flights of fulmars and guillemots wheeling about the steep cliffs. The solitary exposed white egg, faintly spotted lilac around the big end, I took to give to a friend who had asked me for one on the ship which had dropped me off on the Westmann Islands on its way to Iceland. The island boatman offered to keep it safely in the fold of his peaked hat. But, scratching his head as soon as we returned aboard the cod-boat, he forgot about the egg until a yellow streak of yolk oozed over his forehead. (My friend never believed this story.)

Other Studies of Leach's Petrel

Unknown to us at this time, W. A. O. Gross (1935) and our friend Robert Atkinson (Ainslie & Atkinson, 1937) were engaged in a study of Leach's storm petrel, the former where—strangely to us on our treeless windy islands off western coasts of Britain—this bird actually occupies burrows, which it digs in coastal scrub forests on small islands, off the Canadian east coast, north to the Bay of Fundy. These studies, and those of later observers (Huntington, 1953; Wilbur, 1969; Ainley, 1980), show that in general the life-history of *Oceanodroma leucorhoa* closely resembles that of the British storm petrel set out in the first chapters of this book. One principal difference is that it is distributed world-wide in the Pacific, as well as the Atlantic, Ocean. In the Pacific it has developed (subspeciated) into several types or races which, although difficult and often impossible to distinguish at sea, are plain enough when you have them in your hand, either caught alive at their breeding grounds, or 'collected' (shot deliberately as museum specimens).

At sea Atlantic Leach's petrels are easily distinguished from our smaller European storm petrel by their forked tail, longer wings with diagonal pale bar, and more darting and leaping flight. However, it is much harder to separate Leach's from the Madeiran or Harcourt's petrel *O. castro* (of our next chapter), which is almost identical in size. But, as we have seen them following behind ships, the Madeiran has a somewhat squarer, slightly less forked tail. Finer distinctions between the several species of *Oceanodroma* petrels and their races are given in the life-history summaries, page 178.

In studies of Leach's petrel, observers have used stick-lattices to check arrivals and departures at their burrows, but Huntington devised ingenious two-way gates at the burrow entrances, which activate the mercury switches of solenoid-driven markers and record the entry or exit of the birds on sensitised paper.

Leach's storm petrels

The egg (33 × 24mm) is laid about one week after fertile mating. Incubation is shared in shifts of between two and five days. Some nesting material may be brought in (bits of vegetation), but often the egg is laid on the bare earth of the burrow. Incubation averages 40.5 days.

The hatchling, clad in blue-grey down but bare about the neck and head, is nursed continuously for the first five to seven days, when it becomes homoiothermic. The frequency of feeding falls off towards fledging, but larger meals are supplied (by regurgitation). The young bird weighs about one-third more than the adult when it flies to sea at between nine and ten weeks of age. No definite period of parental desertion has been reliably recorded, but the adult moult is well advanced at this time—October. Most of this information is the result of studies at Kent Island, New Brunswick, where Wilbur estimated 15,000 pairs were breeding. Here Huntington and Burtt (1972) find that age at first breeding is five, occasionally four, years, typical of other storm petrels.

In so large a colony there is a considerable inrush of returning birds each summer night soon after dusk; and it is difficult to be sure if there is a regular display flight, as has been suggested for petrels nesting in more open terrain. Undoubtedly most of the circling activity in the air above the trees and scrub at Kent Island is for the purpose of locating the site of the burrow, and making the right approach by dropping to earth through a familiar gap or route through the vegetation. The excited birds 'chatter-call'—a series of harsh notes different from the purring song which usually takes place in the burrow. Sometimes birds collide in the air and may fall to the ground together; it has been suggested that such collisions may be due to a mated pair recognising each other's call—from the evidence of their disappearing below ground together (according to a view held by the late Kenneth Williamson). More certainly there is full partner recognition when the pair meet below ground, by voice—and very likely olfactory clues.

In a homing experiment (Billings, 1968) two Leach's petrels from burrows on Kent Island returned home in 13.7 days when released in Sussex, England—a remarkable performance for such a small bird. It is only a little longer (daily average of at least 350km over the distance of 4,800km) than that of the Manx shearwaters quoted earlier (page 70), travelling in the opposite transatlantic direction. But we have shown that orientation and navigation over what is to man a featureless ocean is an essential ability in sea-wandering species.

Longevity

To date, the oldest banded bird on record had lived twenty-four years. This is comparable with the British storm petrel.

Migration

Leach's petrel is migratory in both its Atlantic and Pacific ranges, wintering far south of the equator. Like our *Hydrobates*, the first-year immatures linger in the tropical belt between 20°N and S of the equator, as proved by specimens taken aboard ships, and those collected for museums. Sightings of fork-tailed, white-rumped, black storm petrels at sea are otherwise bound to be suspect. One Leach's, ringed in Newfoundland in summer and recovered in Spain in January, could have been storm-driven. Occasionally this species suffers considerable 'wrecks' on European coasts after severe and prolonged south-westerly gales. An estimated 7,000 were wrecked on British shores in October–November 1952; many of these were probably from the western Atlantic colonies, since total population of eastern Atlantic colonies, which are limited to small islands off Scotland, the Faeroes and Westmann Islands, and (rather uncertainly) Lofotens, Norway, may not total so many. But in the Newfoundland and other western Atlantic islands there may be several million Leach's breeding.

Geographic Variation

The confusion over the considerable plumage variation in Leach's petrel in the Pacific, which has led 'splitters' among taxonomists to create species and subspecies out of *Oceanodroma leucorhoa*, has been somewhat resolved by D.

G. Ainley (1980), after examining 678 samples from known nesting localities off the west coast of North America. He has merged the subspecies *beali*, *willeti* and *chapmani* into one original *O. leucorhoa*, 'a dichromatic species in which the proportions of color phases and measurable characters vary geographically in a cline, rather than there being a series of distinct populations'. He raises the interesting point from these surveys that the Leach's (and some other storm petrel species), where they breed and feed in 'nearshore' waters, tend to be darker rumped, some with almost no white, than those on islands far offshore.

In the next chapter we consider the all-the-year-round use of burrows on one island, by different species of small petrels, an economy evidently forced by shortage of suitable small islands for successful breeding. But on Guadalupe Island off Lower California, the smallest race of *O. leucorhoa* has evolved, evidently under the same population pressures, into two distinct subspecies which do not interbreed because they have separate breeding seasons. *O. l. socorroensis* completes its activities on land during the four months of summer; but the winter-breeding subspecies, with 'significant differences in five size characters', does not complete nesting and fledging of chicks until some six months later. Ainley therefore proposes the winter-

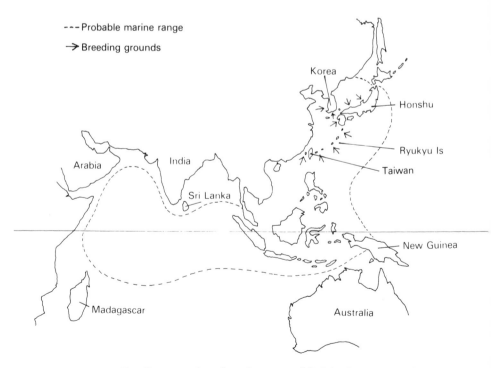

Breeding grounds and marine range of Swinhoe's storm petrel

N.W.C.

Swinhoe's storm petrel

breeding Guadalupe *Oceanodroma leucorhoa* should, on these grounds of 'physiological, morphological and vocal characters', be recognised as a new subspecies, with the proposed name *O. l. cheimomnestes*. Thus are born new subspecies, and eventually species, through isolation of the gene-banks of groups strayed and permanently apart from the parent stock—in this case in time, not geographically.

The general picture of the huge stock of Leach's storm petrel in the Pacific is one of a highly successful superspecies, ranging all temperate coasts, the smaller, all-brown Swinhoe's storm petrel, *O. monorhis*, of the western side and Japan reaching in winter into Indonesian waters and the Indian Ocean. Stragglers have even reached New Zealand; as we go to press Tim Lovegrove and Mike Imber report catching, photographing, banding and releasing two adults found calling near burrows of unrelated species of storm petrels breeding abundantly on Rabbit Island in the Chatham Islands. They were 'typical *O. l. leucorhoa*, behaving suspiciously like potential nesters'. This island hardly offers any room for further burrowing by unestablished species, but if Leach's does get a foothold and breed, it will be the first time known in the southern hemisphere; we may speculate that in a few thousand years it might develop into a distinct species of *Oceanodroma* in such geographical isolation—like the subjects of our next chapter.

9
Madeiran
and other fork-tails

Like the shearwaters and storm petrels of Skokholm, we made a southward journey in summer 1939 along their Atlantic migration route, on another working holiday, while my sister and her husband John Buxton took charge of the island observatory. It was a voyage inspired by new information, gained largely by banding, that both these Skokholm-breeding petrels flew towards the equator, although at that time the extent of their southern migration had not been ascertained.

It was our good fortune to have met, on the Icelandic trip, a merchant of Portugal, Jerry Wright, who had been buying Icelandic klipfish (dried cod) for his Lisbon firm. A keen birdwatcher, from his home in Cascais he arranged the logistics of our visit to several remote Atlantic islands where we might find petrels nesting. In particular, to complete a monograph on shearwaters, I wished to see the mountain-top-breeding Manx shearwaters of Madeira; and secondarily of course we hoped we should find the little-studied Madeiran storm petrel *Oceanodroma castro*.

Madeiran Petrels

Our first sight of this petrel was on 6 July from the stern of the German ss *General San Martin*, bound for Madeira. As we steamed into a cobalt sea beyond the mouth of the yellow Tagus estuary, porpoises rolled and leaped around the ship; and once we had passed out of sight of land, numerous fork-tailed petrels began to follow our wake, skimming and feeding on planktonic matter churned up by our propeller but invisible to us. In flight they appeared almost completely black, compared with the British storm petrel, and a little larger, but with a slightly forked tail—not as forked as the Leach's petrel. The white rump is typical of all three birds, and the pale fringes to the secondary flight feathers are visible as a whitish bar in flight.

To the south-east of the mountainous island of Madeira the long, narrow north–south ridges of the Desertas consist of three steep islands: Chao, the most northerly, is distantly in sight of the port of Funchal. They were formerly inhabited, but are now abandoned. When we landed by dinghy

Madeiran storm petrel

from a steam tender at Chao on 10 July, we found the island a desert of volcanic soil and rubble, in which grew a few drought-resistant plants. Some sparse grass had the appearance of hay, grazed by a few large, sandy-coloured rabbits. The iceplant *Mesembryanthemum cristallinum* struggled over much of the waterless 100 acre plateau, its globular leaves full of a colourless liquid. We camped on Chao, where we found the shade temperature almost constant at 23 °C, a refreshing medium warmth, owing to the constant north-east trade wind which never ceased to blow out of a sky without overhead clouds. Chao was in fact a delightful island whose plateau we had altogether to ourselves; a few fishermen remained by night in a little creek 60 metres below the steep cliffs, up which we had had some difficulty in hoisting our tent, water, gear and other stores. We decided to remain as long as possible, studying its wild life. Despite its arid appearance, we watched canaries, pipits, swifts, kestrel and buzzard, common tern and the yellow-legged herring gull.

There were four tubenoses breeding. The large North Atlantic shear-water *Puffinus (Calonectris) diomedea*, and the all-black Bulwer's petrel *Bulweria bulwerii* are both unfortunately hunted as food by the ever-hungry impoverished Madeiran fishermen. Cut-off petrel wings were lying around middens heaped with limpet shells, near the landing place. Safer from this predation, because they are small and nest in less accessible crevices, are the other two: the charming allied or little shearwater *Puffinus assimilis*, a miniature kind of Manx shearwater; and *Oceanodroma castro*.

We set up camp within a roofless stone hut, relic of a former habitation, and slung our tent high as an awning. This delighted innumerable lizards which ran over the surface, climbed guy wires, and darted into our food store. By the time we had made this lizard-proof, it was dark. The lizards retired into crevices in the rock walls, and presently there were strange night noises, of the new petrels we had come to study. Loudest was the sobbing cry of the cagarra, so named by the Madeiran fishermen from its harsh wailing—this was Cory's or the North Atlantic great shearwater. A repeated

Little shearwater

low note, 'Wow', came from the heaped-up stones near the hut, from a nesting colony of perhaps twenty pairs of Bulwer's petrel. This is as large as a large blackbird, quite black, with a long wedge-shaped tail and yellow-brown legs down to about one-third of the webbing of its feet, the toes and claws being black.

We slung our fine-mesh bird-net between the hut and this cairn of stones, and soon caught and banded nineteen Bulwer's petrels. Seven were later traced to crevices and found to be incubating eggs close to hatching. Two chicks in fact hatched during our stay. As this fine bird is not a storm petrel, it hardly concerns this book. But it was interesting to find that the new-born chick was very different, and highly precocious, compared with our almost helpless Skokholm storm chicks. It was born with its eyes open, in a profuse black down about 12mm long; and when, within a few hours of hatching, one was experimentally placed in the open on the rocks it immediately began hooking its way with bill and claws and tiny wing-stumps back into cover. There was no bald spot on the crown. Obviously, we thought, the high temperature of this latitude encouraged this liveliness.

Amid the barking 'wows' of Bulwer's, which at a distance sounded like a hound which had lost its way in some far ravine, we heard a soft squeaking note. I found it could be closely imitated by rubbing a finger hard on glass, a sound vaguely like the rarer call of our Skokholm petrel on the wing, which however is much softer. Numbers of Madeiran petrels were flying about in the darkness, revealed as white-rumped fairy-like flashes passing through the beam of our torch. But few seemed to be settling into holes, as traceable by the call. Most of them flew high, between 3 and 30 metres overhead. By day we scrambled about wherever there were loose rocks and talus, and along dry-stone boundary walls of the former farm, listening and sniffing for petrels. We located one pair crooning together in a crevice, from which we extracted them with the fine wire crook, banded and returned them. There was no egg; the pair were evidently courting, their song a purr resembling that of the British storm petrel, softer, with the window-pane squeak thrown in at intervals; it was altogether tantalising to try to record these noises phonetically on paper (no handy tape recorders at that time).

Those few days and nights on Chao passed all too quickly, bird-watching in our desert-island paradise. To the south lay the larger ridge of Deserta Grande. One evening we persuaded Manoel, the young fisherman guide we had engaged at Funchal (he lived with the other fishermen in their camp at Chao landing-place) to ferry us to this arid mountain rising over 600 metres from the sea. Our adventures in crossing the sound between in a fresh wind and an inadequate dinghy have been described in the book *Shearwaters*. But

Madeiran storm petrel outside its rocky crevice

it had to be at night, climbing that almost sheer cliff path, because the shearwaters and storm petrels are then most active on land, visiting their burrows only during darkness.

We were told that the Desertas are vivid in spring with poppies and other wild flowers, but on that midsummer night of 11 July Grande lived up to its name, a desert eroded by wind and goats, its larger birds hunted and slaughtered (many severed wings of shearwaters) by hungry visiting fishermen, as at Chao. We toiled upwards over the dry rock slopes, finding only a few petrels to catch and band. At the peak, about 1,600ft (457m), it was cold with the north wind; fortunately we discovered some clumps of dead gorse with which to fuel a fire at midnight and revive our chilled bodies. My diary notes:

> Grande is disappointing from its lack of birds, a place of dried yellow grass and stones with a rare clump of wormwood, more God-forsaken and desolate than our lowly, lovely Chao. The fishermen have driven most of the petrels to inaccessible nesting places in the cliffs, from which we heard their various calls, including the squeak of the Madeiran stormie.
>
> At five o'clock dawn was breaking. We made our way back to the dinghy, moored in the surf a thousand feet below. A few pipits ran before us, a buzzard soared into the air with dark Madeiran swifts leaving their rock homes in the cliffs, a goat and some rabbits scampered from the steep path. . . . We were happy to get back—a toilsome row of one hour for Manoel against the wind—to Chao landing. Here five ragged fishermen were eating a breakfast of sweet potatoes and limpets boiled over a fire of wormwood sticks. Their little boat is hardly the length of our *Storm Petrel*. Probably they enjoy this life as much as the Pembrokeshire fishermen used to do when we first visited Skokholm. At least they are reasonably free men, living on what they can catch along the wild shore. As we climbed up the cliff ravine to our camp we surprised another two men into releasing a rabbit they had snared, evidently alarmed we might (Manoel later told us) report them to the owner of Chao (Hinton of Funchal) from whom we had obtained permission to camp. The fishermen were living at Chao only by traditional right, which in the circumstances meant that they were poaching— and knew it! Poor fishermen—as if we would betray them!

Almost reluctantly we abandoned our study of Chao petrels when the *Butio* called to take us a few days later to the Selvagens which, although 180 miles south of Madeira and nearer the Spanish-owned Canary Islands, are a Portuguese possession. The little steamer was filled with Madeiran labourers on the lower deck, and on the 'bridge deck', a hen-coop arrangement with an awning, were 'the passengers'—ourselves and some Funchal gentlemen out for a cruise and a rabbit hunt. It was a calm day, the steamer rocked gently to the blue swell, we listed the birds seen (only a few storm petrels) which included a Kentish plover and great and sooty shear-waters; and admired the leaping and gliding of flying fish.

We arrived at the open unlighted Selvagens anchorage, by clever piloting in the darkness, at 1 a.m. The one main island is a plateau of about 400 acres, showing signs of former human occupation in stone boundary walls as at Chao (possibly a penal settlement), but there are no houses. The labourers live in natural caves near the landing ravine, and contract to dig and bag the phosphatic soil which covers the top of the island. This is really guano, mixed with volcanic dust, accumulated over centuries of breeding and burrowing by sea birds. The island is largely a vast 'cagarra' farm, dominated by some 20,000 pairs of these North Atlantic great shearwaters. As they are unmolested during the breeding season, they are tame and partly diurnal, arriving from the sea from late afternoon onwards. When the fat young are ready to fly in the autumn, up to two-thirds are collected and salted for human consumption in Madeira.

The skipper of the *Butio* warned us that we must return to the boat as soon as he sounded the siren, which he would do when the cargo of guano was loaded, or earlier if a swell got up and made the anchorage unsafe. We spent the whole time—about forty hours—observing and banding every petrel we could lay hands on. We had already worked out at Chao the incubation shifts shared by male and female Bulwer's petrels, plentiful also on Selvagens; and now—as far as the limited time allowed—we tried to do the same for the cagarra. This was made easy because along the foot of the old stone boundary walls, stones had been pulled out to leave shallow nesting cavities at intervals of about 1 metre, for convenience of collecting the fledgelings in the autumn.

On the level plateau during the day labourers were digging and sacking; each full bag of soil was carried shoulder-high the half-mile to the tiny harbour. This digging destroyed many nests of three small petrels.

Sharing the Year—and the Space

This plateau area was pitted and riddled with small holes and burrows in which were breeding the little shearwater, the Madeiran storm petrel, and a new bird for us, the white-faced or frigate storm petrel *Pelagodroma marina*. With so many of each species killed by the digging operations, it was easy for us to discover that here the territorial year must be divided up so that the limited accommodation is shared with the least possible competition. Most of the Madeiran storm petrels had laid their egg; some were fresh and transparent-looking, others opaque with a developing chick, when held up against the light. The handsome little shearwaters were at the courtship stage, flying about and crooning on the ground at night, but none had laid eggs, and few remained in the burrows during daylight. But the dainty white-breasted frigate petrels (see next chapter) had almost completed breeding; the guano-diggers uncovered their well-feathered chicks with

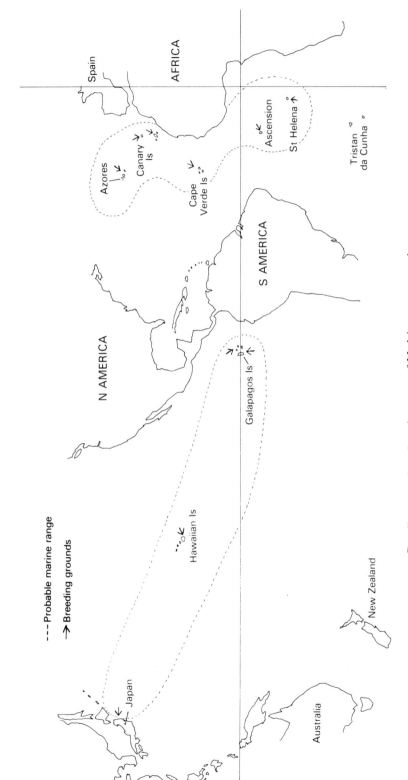

--- Probable marine range
➤ Breeding grounds

N AMERICA

S AMERICA

AFRICA

Spain

Azores

Canary
Is

Cape
Verde Is

Ascension

St Helena

Tristan
da Cunha

Galapagos Is

Hawaiian Is

Japan

New Zealand

Australia

Breeding grounds and marine range of Madeiran storm petrel

little down left, and threw these away—to be devoured by a small group of yellow-legged gulls which daily attended the workers for this free hand-out.

Overlapping must occur, but it seemed clear to us that the honeycombed ground was economically shared by the frigate petrel, occupying the burrows from April to July, the Madeiran stormies from July to December, and the little shearwater, which elsewhere is a winter breeder, taking up the winter third of the reproductive year. It is only on such temperate or tropical islands as the Selvagens, remote and generally uninhabited, that there is freedom from human interference, a suitable terrain for burrowing, and a winter climate mild enough for birds which have comparatively short nesting seasons to share the accommodation in this economical manner.

Mike Harris, ex-Skokholm warden, discusses this sharing of site and year by *Oceanodroma* species in the Galapagos Islands. There is quite fierce competition for the limited nest sites, not only between species but also intraspecifically between groups of the same species. He confirms what Dr David Snow and his wife found in their studies on the Galapagos, that two entirely separate populations of *O. castro* nest in the same burrows here, one in the warm season, the other during the cold. This separation applied equally to immature birds returned to the island for the first time; there was no mingling or visiting of individuals to break the isolation of each group.

The Madeiran petrel, more usually known as Harcourt's storm petrel in the Pacific, is tropical and sub-tropical in its breeding and feeding range. In the Galapagos group it nests on some ten small islets off the larger human-inhabited islands, the requirements for survival being the absence of predatory mammals. It has to suffer some predation from the resident owl *Asio flammeus galapagoensis*, but this does not seriously deplete the population. Intraspecific competition for burrows is one factor reducing breeding success, as elsewhere; and on Isla Pitt the very large colony of the resident Galapagos storm petrel, *Oceanodroma tethys*, apparently inhibits *O. castro* from breeding during the cold season by occupying all the available nesting sites; this is known as interspecific competition.

The same fierce struggle to obtain suitable nesting sites is described between individual Madeiran storm-petrel adults at Ascension Island in the South Atlantic. On the small rat-free Boatswain's Islet, Stonehouse (1960) records that five or six marked adults fought for the limited accommodation of one nesting recess—'a housing shortage, and this we helped to remedy by providing nest-boxes, designed with a glass cover under the lid and a tunnel entrance four or five inches long; each one was partly buried in guano dust so that the entrance closely resembled a tiny cavity in the rock. The petrels took to them most satisfactorily, and were soon turning each other out as though every box were a cherished ancestral home. Eggs were laid early in October. With so many birds scuffling for each hole it was not surprising that some of the earliest layers lost their nests during the first stages of incubation. As always, the first act of the usurping pair was to tidy up, and a number of freshly-laid eggs appeared among the refuse at the burrow entrances.'

Breeding Biology

The Madeiran storm petrel prefers rocky crevices in which to lay its single white egg. Like other storm-petrel eggs it is zoned near the big end with fine pink spots which gradually fade during incubation. Average size is 32 × 24mm, weight 8–9g. The Madeiran petrel follows the pattern of our Skokholm petrel in almost all respects. Incubation takes forty-two days and is shared by both parents in shifts of up to a week. The fledging period averages about sixty-six days; the fledgeling is fed less frequently towards the end, and not at all during the last couple of days before it flies away to sea. The unhatched egg, in the warmer climate, has an even longer resistance to chilling; Harris records one embryo of *O. castro* 'remaining alive for 23 days without incubation, while a chick inside a chipping *O. tethys* egg continued to call for 16 days'.

There is the same faithfulness of the established breeder to mate and nest, so universal in these little petrels. Also, first return to the natal colony is

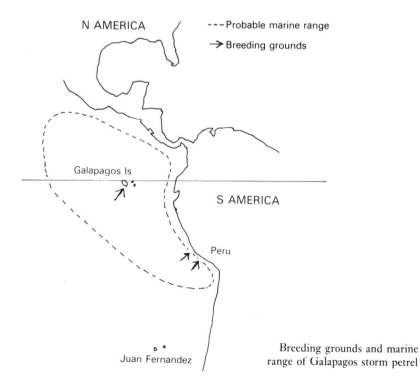

Breeding grounds and marine range of Galapagos storm petrel

Galapagos storm petrels

unusual before two years of age, and successful establishment as a breeder is rarely before, and sometimes later than, five years. The moult of adults takes place immediately after breeding; and in the immatures, as for British and Wilson's storm petrels, first moult is a more leisurely affair extending over the first long year at sea.

Galapagos Storm Petrel *Oceanodroma tethys*

It will be appropriate here to deal with this competitor for nest sites with the Madeiran species, described above. Although slightly smaller than the Madeiran, *O. tethys* returns from its night-feeding activities by day, about the only known storm petrel to do so. 'Unbelievable numbers'—at least several hundreds of thousands as seen by several observers—arrive on their main breeding grounds in the cliffs and lava fields of isolated Tower Island, where Harris (1969) mist-netted many, but circumstances prevented him from maintaining a watch on marked burrows to cover the whole incubation and fledging period. The colonies were too overcrowded; up to twenty-two eggs and five young were found under one lava bubble in the rocks in 1967, yet 'no more than five young could have fledged from this hole in 1966'.

Obviously the limiting factor is this intense competition for nesting places for safe rearing—as safe at least as this sedentary petrel can find within its range, a few hundred kilometres around the Galapagos group, and eastwards to the Peruvian coast. When passing through the Galapagos by steamer in 1961, we found *O. tethys* fairly easy to identify at sea from its extensive white rump. Harris watched them in broad daylight flighting over the nesting ground. The movement was bouncing and tern-like—just as one imagines most storm petrels must move when approaching a nesting crevice by night. Some alighted several times, in different places, without going below ground; some ran nimbly along the ground, with spread wings and tail, but others ran with their wings closed. He suggests that the smell of regurgitated oil drew some birds to alight and peck briefly at the spot. He concludes: 'The very conspicuous white rump patch appears to be important in both aerial and terrestrial displays. As well as being used as a signal to other birds of the same species, it might conceivably serve as a deflective mark to attract a predator's attention to a nonvital part of the body. Associated with this is the relative ease with which the upper-tail coverts are pulled out.'

There is always a reason for colour or pattern in nature; but, it may be noted, several storm petrels are perfectly brown, or black, all over. Moving north in the Pacific, we find three all-dark *Oceanodroma* species.

Ashy Storm Petrel *Oceanodroma homochroa*

19cm (7.5in). Small, sooty-coloured, with short legs and forked tail. Could be mistaken for the black storm petrel (page 182), which is larger and with more forked tail. Confined to breeding along the outer coast of California in summer. Little studied and rather scarce. On the few islands where it breeds it is strictly nocturnal because of western gulls which hunt them by day.

Ashy storm petrels

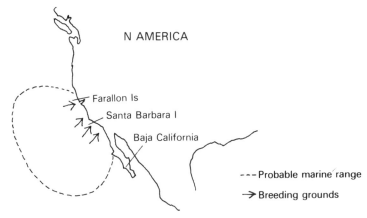

N AMERICA

Farallon Is

Santa Barbara I

Baja California

--- Probable marine range

→ Breeding grounds

Breeding grounds and marine range of ashy storm petrel

Tristram's Storm Petrel *Oceanodroma tristrami*

23–25cm (9–10in). Wingspan 56cm. Large, all-brown, with deeply forked tail. Almost swallow-like in flight over the sea. A winter breeder on the Leeward Hawaiian Islands. Bonin and Torishima in the Izu Islands.

Tristram's storm petrel

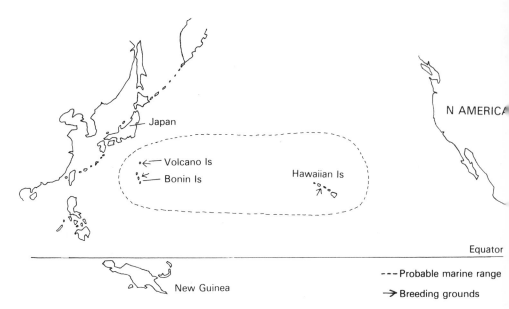

Breeding grounds and marine range of Tristram's storm petrel

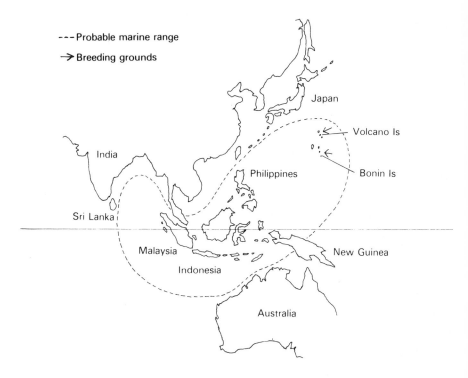

Breeding grounds and marine range of Matsudaira's storm petrel

Matsudaira's Storm Petrel *Oceanodroma matsudairae*

25cm (10in). Very like Tristram's petrel, but with whitish shafts to the primary wing-feathers. Its distribution does not overlap with that of Tristram's, but is similar to that of Swinhoe's storm petrel. Nests on the Volcano Islands south of Japan and reaches the Indian Ocean during the non-breeding season.

Matsudaira's storm petrel

Oceanodroma of the Northern Snows

The scene shifts to the far north, into sub-Arctic and Bering Sea islands, as far towards the snow and ice as storm petrels are known to feed and breed. In the late summer of 1978 I took a pack on my back and made my way through the sounds of British Columbia north to Alaska, to Barrow on the Arctic Ocean, and lived for a while with Eskimos on St Lawrence Island in the north Bering Sea, and with Aleuts on the Pribilof Islands.

My main object was to see Arctic whales and dolphins and complete a book on cetaceans for my publishers. Most of each day, travelling from Vancouver by steamer to Juneau, we were in sight of whales and dolphins, especially the splendid orca (misnamed the killer whale), feeding on the

Fork-tailed storm petrels

abundant salmon or on the smaller fish and krill eaten by the salmon. This inside passage was a wonderful experience, passing through fiords whose steep banks were clothed in conifers where brown bears roamed, at that July season sampling the wild strawberries and other fruits along this flowery shore strewn with stranded logs. At intervals little flocks of storm petrels fluttered near the ship; but they were too difficult to identify certainly, having white rumps. Most of them were 'probably Leach's storm petrel', as I cautiously noted in my diary.

In sight of the Queen Charlotte Islands (where I landed and stayed a few days to look at the large bald-eagle population, among other new delights) the few fork-tailed petrels seemed much lighter than Leach's, and were 'probably a new species to me, *Oceanodroma furcata*; but can't be sure. This petrel, known as *the* fork-tailed storm petrel, is the same size as Leach's, but its flight is said to be different. The trouble is, the southern subspecies is about as dark as Leach's.'

However, cruising in the sheltered waters of Glacier Bay, north of Juneau, with the Charles Jurasz family, studying humpback whales from their house-boat *Jinjur*, we had good views of the paler northern subspecies of *O. furcata*, a few of which were mingling with larger numbers of Leach's. With thousands of phalaropes, auks, gulls and terns, they were greedily feeding on the swarming plankton and tiny 'seed' capelin, along with humpback and minke whales. I have never seen such a wonderful

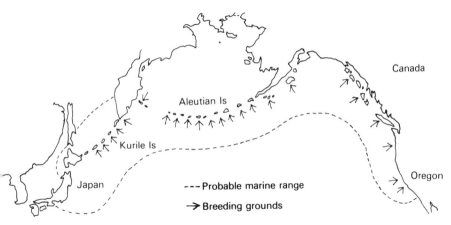

Breeding grounds and marine range of fork-tailed storm petrel

concentration of sea creatures, so vividly presented against a background of North America's highest mountains, with glaciers at sea-level. The chattering of the sea birds was interrupted by the loud blasts of whales spouting nearby. A bald eagle dived upon a gull struggling with a large fish at the surface and robbed it with a plunging swoop of its talons. The *Jinjur* motored quietly, or drifted silently among the rapidly melting ice floes; even hooked to one to obtain fresh ice for our evening drinks . . . Perfection of living for those few days!

Not many days later I reached St Lawrence Island by small plane from the little city of Nome, once a gold-rush centre, reduced to 3,000 inhabitants and now quaintly touristic. Talking with the hospitable Eskimo family who put me up on the cold windy Bering Sea island, which is closer to Siberia than Alaska, I learned that the only storm petrel they knew was (to translate its Eskimo name) 'the oil-eater'. These friendly islanders speak the Siberian 'Yupik' dialect, and live by hunting Arctic whales (bowhead, gray and white), walrus, migrant seals, and (in winter) polar bears, with much fishing and sea-bird fowling in summer. Mid-July was a good time to visit, at the height of the Bering Sea late spring. My diary records:

20 July, 0900 hours. In a six-seater plane flying at 4,500ft above the Bering Sea in the co-pilot seat, speed 155mph, distance $1\frac{1}{4}$ hours and 170 nautical miles to St Lawrence. The young pilot, having warned us not to smoke, has just lit a cigarette. Low white cloud and almost calm sea below us. The pilot says this is a very fine day; if it is foggy he can usually get down on the island by a combination of time, compass bearing and directional radio cross-bearings—no radar fitted. Descending after an hour reveals a long island with many lakes, and patches of snow down to sea level. We land smoothly on a narrow tarseal strip in the glacial gravel where the stark village of Gambel stands, with naked framehouses and wooden racks on which hang skins and strips of meat swinging in a cool misty sunlight.

Willy-nilly, I am snatched up by a famous hunting Eskimo whose English

name is 'Winnie' James. I cannot argue, but it seems there is competition to be
hospitable. I should have been picked up by one Tim Slowooko, the Wien Air
agent to whom I had an introduction. Never mind, this is an exciting place, and
Winnie whisks me away astride the back of his Honda three-wheeler, fat-tyred
runabout which people use here to go anywhere over shingle or bog, at alarming
speeds. Most islanders have husky dogs, but no longer drive dog-sledges. They
have skidoos (motorised toboggans), in which they travel far when hunting over
the winter ice of the Bering Sea. 'You name Ronald?' said Winnie James. 'OK.
When they put us top Yupik hunters in special commando corps during war,
recruiting sergeant ask my name. I say Aningayou. Sergeant roll eyes, can't speak
Yupik. He say OK, no good. He write down next best thing—Winifred James.
OK I say. So now white man know me as Winnie James.'

We arrived at a ramshackle wooden framehouse which nevertheless had TV
(very poor), bathroom-loo (no water), table loaded with drinks (chiefly whisky)
for the old, and sweets and chocolate for the young, and other useful and useless
status symbols of modern Eskimo society. They are affluent even here, having
had a large hand-out from Uncle Sam as their share of compensation for Alaska's
oil wealth taken over by the USA government; but they do well from the sale of
furs and their beautiful carvings in ivory from walrus tusks, mostly dug up from
the middens of 3,000 years of Eskimo occupation of the island.

His stocky wife Kulukhon (Anna) fried some fresh seal meat, basted with seal
blood, over the modern electric stove. It was delicious to my hungry palate. Their
eldest son Urregu presented me with a fossil penial walrus bone, which he said I
could have 'Very cheap, only $100, worth double in New York . . .'

Rather sadly the use of Eskimo names is dying out, even the language is
spoken less. English names are given or chosen by children when they first
attend the Gambel school. Anna and James had a happy lot around them,
who pen-printed their names in my diary: Urregu (James junior), Uugalog
(Dennis), Seppelu (Sally), Nannita (Veronica), Tutemquiilngug (Elsie),
Annaalnggha (Gloria), and Nuut (April).

James was a great bird expert—chiefly with the gun. He would take me to
some bird-cliff or marsh, riding several miles on the back of his big-tyred
motor-tricycle, his rifle slung over his back and squeezed against my chest as
I clung to his belt and bounced up and down. He thought the little petrel,
the oil-eater, nested deep in the tumbled screes on the north side, and here
he dumped me for a day. He knew it best at sea when hunting whales, walrus
and seal among the floating ice. For it came fearlessly to snatch up its share
of the kill, swallowing bits of flesh, clots of blood, and any fatty oily fluid
floating on the water, sometimes hovering over the ice with dangling feet to
do so. This scavenging habit has been noted of *Oceanodroma furcata* by
several observers: on 17 September, Robert Gill (1977) saw this fork-tailed
petrel feeding on the beached remains of a gray whale *Eschrichtius robustus*
which had been trapped by ice and died the previous April at Nelson
Lagoon, Alaska peninsula. The weather was rough at the time, but the bird
sometimes landed on the shore, and also on the whale, in order to pick up

these titbits. This bird was collected and proved to be a female. Her stomach contents included whale fat, feathers, fish eye-lens and pieces of pumice (the last probably picked up floating at sea). Gill writes: 'This observation is of note because it provides direct evidence of a terrestrial (ie non-pelagic) foraging capability by *O. furcata*. It also furthers the scant knowledge on the use of beached marine mammals for food by pelagic and inshore avifauna, especially during adverse weather when normal foraging habits might be inhibited.'

Ornithologists have called this opportunistic feeding 'local enhancement'; it occurs commonly in Wilson's petrel (next chapter) at whale-flensing stations in South Georgia. (Hunger may be the principal reason why many storm petrels and other birds commonly swallow small stones and vegetation-stalk of no nutritional value. Seal and sea-lion species ingest stones, probably for a like reason.)

It was exciting to wander along the steep slopes of this wild Eskimo island where thousands of sea birds were nesting, some new species for me — large-horned puffins, and the little rhinoceros-horned auklets, which seemed to be sharing innumerable holes and rock crevices with a subspecies of the Arctic lemming. The lower slopes near the sea were the home of black guillemots; and everywhere pairs of snow-buntings, the cocks singing or carrying food to nests hidden under fallen stones. High up, close to hollows still full of winter snow, ruddy turnstones were running with very small chicks, and godwits passed overhead. To crown this vast bounty of bird life, the whole rock slope was a beautiful garden of low-growing Arctic and sub-Arctic wild flowers: coltsfoot, roseroot, white saxifrage, pink lousewort, anemone, oxeye daisy, blue aconite (monkshood), meadow rue, fritillary, rubus—these are the names I noted in my diary, but without collecting any; just admiring their loveliness against moss and lichen-covered stones a good deal splashed with the mutings of the auks and auklets, which make this ancient summer home of the sea birds such a fertile garden. Delving and listening at small holes and rock crevices I could find no storm petrels. Now and then a lemming ran between one burrow and another. Spent cartridge-cases attested the visits of Eskimo wildfowlers to these vast 'loomeries' of the edible sea birds.

Five days later I reached the Pribilof Islands, now a seal and sea-otter reserve, southward in the Bering Sea (57°S, 170°W), a much warmer, though still treeless, group. The low undulating plateau of Saint Paul Island is lush and colourful in July with yellow Arctic poppy, tall delicate pink lousewort, and a kind of angelica, in which moulting fur seals can sometimes be found fast asleep some distance inland from the assembly beaches. The steep cliffs above the seal beaches have a wonderful array of nesting birds which I have no room to describe here. The pale-winged *furcata* fork-tailed storm petrel was frequently seen feeding close inshore amid hundreds of fur seals arriving from, or leaving for, the open sea, or merely washing and splashing lazily in the smooth swell under a hazy sky. Possibly the storm petrels were picking up scraps of oily, fishy matter excreted by the seals, or planktonic life, or both. Many larger sea birds were flying between the cliffs and the sea: thick-billed murres, crested and horned puffins, least and crested auklets, red-legged kittiwake gulls, the handsome red-faced cormorant, and the graceful Pacific fulmar.

The Aleutian fishermen of St Paul believed that storm petrels were nesting on some offshore islets around the southern island of St George. There was no chance to verify this; but it is interesting that the first specimen of *O. furcata* known to science (as far as I can trace) was collected during Captain James Cook's last voyage, 1778–9, from north of the Bering Strait; and evidently it forages right into the Arctic Ocean when the whales, walrus, and many sea birds seek the rich late summer sea-food close to the melting pack-ice.

Farthest traveller of this fleet of marine creatures surging through the Bering Strait to the ice limits in the Arctic and Beaufort seas in late summer is the world's greatest long-distance migrant tubenose, the slender-billed shearwater *Puffinus tenuirostris*. As mentioned in a later chapter, I had studied it for a while on small islands off Tasmania, where it nests in burrows, and has a breeding biology that is almost the counterpart of our Skokholm shearwater. And now here it was! Small flocks were to be seen daily in the sea around Pribilof St Paul, along with *furcata* petrels.

The wonder and mystery of that accurate navigation of thousands of miles of open ocean by low-flying, southern hemisphere shearwaters came to me vividly, as I watched those long wings gliding and gyrating gracefully over these cool northern waters. Had I not handled and admired some individuals which at that moment, like me, had come so far from our Antipodean homes? The Pribilof men said matter-of-factly that these southern shearwaters swarmed here in summer—they shot the 'alamach' for food when fishing at sea, but the 'okuik' (oil-eater) was too small to eat.

Yes, I mused, Captain Cook first saw this shearwater when he rediscovered in 1777 Van Diemen's Land (Tasmania)—where immense flocks frequent the Bass Strait—and he must have seen thousands here in the Bering Sea. He and his men had also seen Wilson's, the most southern storm petrel in the world, amid the icebergs of the Antarctic Ocean, and he, or one of his men, had seen (and shot) the most northern, the fork-tailed *furcata*, too, near the pack ice of the Arctic Ocean. And now so had I—but without the shooting . . .

Modern studies of *O. f. furcata* nesting in the Aleutians have revealed a life story closely resembling Wilson's (next chapter), on a general pattern common to all the hydrobatids. On the Barren Islands, about 550km south-south-west from Anchorage, T. R. Simons (1981) monitored a number of burrows by placing a clear plastic window and plywood cover over the nesting chamber with a two-way switch enclosed in a section of plastic pipe above the burrow entrance. This neat 'event recorder' registered the visits of the adults which were colour-marked to establish identity. Seven marked nests were followed in 1977, and six in 1978. In addition a marked pair within an exposed burrow were kept under observation from a blind (hide), using a night vision telescope.

O. furcata arrives in the Aleutians in April. Egg-laying begins as soon as the winter snow melts and uncovers the established burrows, generally on the higher ground first. Deep drifts at sea level take longer to melt. As in Wilson's petrel, toleration of chilling of the embryo in the egg is high, an adaptation for survival in an environment where storms are severe and unpredictable, and food resources resultantly variable. In the same islands Boersma & Wheelwright (1979) found the mean number of days of egg neglect in 33 nests was 11. Fortunately burrow temperatures averaged 10°C. This neglect extended the incubation period by the number of days of adult absence; with continuous brooding the egg hatches about the forty-first day, as in Leach's petrel.

The male initiates nesting by calling with a single 'sex-specific' note from the burrow; a rasping five-syllable call is used apparently,by either sex, uttered from the burrow, and also in flight overhead. Courtship preening and copulation occurs in the burrow; incubation is shared in approximately equal shifts of one to five days. The pair meet at night during the changeover, when there is chattering and preening which strengthens the pair bond. One adult in the observation nest was seen assisting the hatching chick by placing its bill inside the partly opened shell, and shaking its head from side to side as if impatient; but could the action instead have been part of tender loving care?

The fledging period averages fifty-eight or fifty-nine days, and although the fat fledgeling is not fed in the last few days, and begins to lose weight, the adults may still visit the burrow, even for a day or two after the young bird has flown. But it should be remembered that this storm petrel is almost non-migratory, only moving away from its Bering Sea and Aleutian home when driven south by winter snow and ice. Three fledgelings which were observed to leave their burrows early after dark returned a number of times before departing before midnight. (An observation showing the value of the sophisticated equipment which Simons used in recording natural behaviour—if only I had had a 'night vision scope' in those early nights of petrel-watching at Skokholm!)

Oceanodroma furcata, among the eleven true species (discounting subspecies) of this genus, is unmistakable at sea by its unique pearl-grey or blue-grey upper parts, dark eye-area, faint grey, nearly white under parts, the flanks and under-tail coverts white. In flight I thought it looked rather like a miniature fulmar petrel with a forked tail, gliding somewhat like (and with) that relative, but with wings more angled, almost white in sunshine at a distance. But in the often misty weather of the Bering Sea it was a beautiful pale blue-grey with white flashes of under-wing and flanks.

The breeding grounds of two larger fork-tailed *Oceanodroma* petrels are as yet virtually undiscovered.

Markham's Storm Petrel *Oceanodroma markhami*

23–25cm (9–10in). Wingspan 56cm. Indistinguishable at sea from Tristram's, except that it ranges a different oceanic zone, chiefly off the coast of Peru. It is remarkable that the breeding grounds are still quite unknown. Females with fully formed eggs in their oviducts have been taken off the coast of Peru, where they flight and feed with other *Oceanodroma* storm petrels. Murphy suggests that Markham's petrel may nest on small rocky islets, or else inland in the High Andes, like the next.

Markham's storm petrel

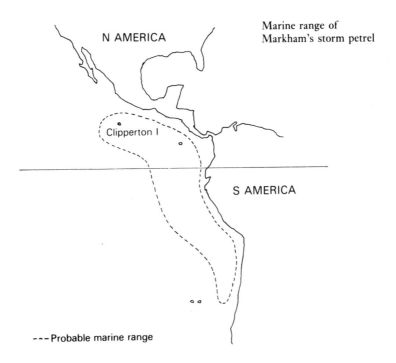

N AMERICA

Marine range of
Markham's storm petrel

Clipperton I

S AMERICA

- - - Probable marine range

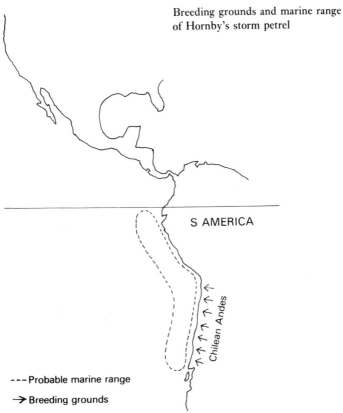

Breeding grounds and marine range
of Hornby's storm petrel

S AMERICA

Chilean Andes

- - - Probable marine range

→ Breeding grounds

Hornby's storm petrels

Hornby's Storm Petrel *Oceanodroma hornbyi*

20–23cm (8–9in). Another mysterious west coast of South America (Humboldt Current) storm petrel. Johnson, in *Birds of Chile* (1965), gives the following records which indicate that this medium-large, distinctly plumaged petrel nests in the High Andes of Peru and Chile. In 1894 a full-grown chick, with some down visible, was taken from a hole in the coastal hills above the port of Taltal (now in Santiago National Museum). In 1923 mummified specimens of nestlings were discovered in holes in the Loa River canyon where it crosses the nitrate desert inland from Tocopilla. In the same year another mummified specimen was found in the Santa Luisa de Taltal nitrate fields 30 miles from the coast at an altitude of 5,000ft (1,521 metres). Lastly, Johnson records that Dr Koepcke and his wife 'have recently caught several specimens of this petrel at night in the streets of Lima, Peru. Some of these still had abundant patches of down on the abdomen, showing conclusively that they must have been hatched somewhere near at hand.' Evidently these are young birds from burrows in the high Andes. On their first flight to the sea, they have been forced down by bad weather and dazzled by the street lights—a not infrequent hazard.

A little smaller than Markham's, Hornby's storm petrel is grey on its upper parts rather than black, the upper wings are darker and there is a distinct brown cap set like a monk's pate-covering back on the head. Forehead, cheeks, chin, throat, upper breast and belly are white, with a clean brown-grey band across the breast.

Wilson's storm petrel

'Ocean sprite of the oceans!' Well named is *Oceanites oceanicus*, this small storm petrel, 180mm long from bill-tip to end of square tail, which makes one of the greatest transocean voyages of all birds. It is certainly the hardiest small bird in the world in its breeding habits, nesting close to the South Pole, and frequently snowed in and entombed as a result. Yet it was claimed by James Fisher (Fisher & Lockley, 1954) to be the most numerous sea bird, if not the most numerous of all birds, in the world. You may see it as far north in the Atlantic as Newfoundland and South of Greenland, where we have watched its wonderfully graceful water-pattering flight; and only a few months ago we saw it feeding on krill as far south as man may take a ship in Antarctica. Off the Cape of Good Hope we have watched it mingling with our northern-breeding storm petrels. In the Pacific Ocean, where it was once believed to be rather scarce, it is now known to reach the equator during the southern hemisphere winter.

It is easily recognised at sea by its size, square tail, white rump and very long legs dangling from an otherwise wholly black body. Characteristically the long legs extend beyond the tail during fast flight; but when the bird is feeding the long feet lightly touch the water, and the webs are seen to be yellow. If you know your petrels well enough at sea, the flight of the Wilson's petrel is distinctly lighter than that of other small storm petrels: that is, it seemed to us to be more airy, or aerial, and bounding, with frequent leaps several metres high. The Tristan da Cunha islanders know it as the skipjack bird. When it is intent on feeding, Robert Cushman Murphy's description fits well—a series of short glides interspersed with fluttering and hovering, with legs toe-dancing over the surface.

Wilson's storm petrel is both solitary and gregarious, often encountered alone, or in flocks of hundreds, even of thousands, concentrating on its normal planktonic food. It freely attends fishing ships which are gutting their catch, and like many other petrels, will follow the wake of a fast-moving ship for the sake of organisms churned up by the propeller. It will snatch up the almost invisible scraps of blood, flesh and oil too small for the gulls, skuas and larger scavenging petrels during whale-flensing operations as this material reaches the sea from a ship or land-processing base. It has been recorded as hawking after flying insects. It is adept at hovering in one

Wilson's storm petrel

spot, even moving backwards in a strong wind, when intent on feeding.

Watching their scavenging habits at South Georgia in November 1912, Murphy (1936) declared that the resident skuas—'wanton relentless ogres'—which killed larger birds, ignored Wilson's petrel so long as it was not dead or disabled. (The truth is a healthy adult is too nimble on the wing.) He found them quite noisy at sea where they gathered after sunset with other petrels in 'myriads, their numbers revealed by a chorus of twittering and the soft unbroken sound of winnowing quills'. You may hear this peeping and winnowing murmur if you are close to a flock of these petrels feeding excitedly at sea; and a variety of these high-pitched squeaks, and some lower, more grating cries, can be heard by night at the breeding sites. They are, like the conversation of gnomes and fairies, too difficult to translate into words!

As a young ardent bird-watcher I had thought that Wilson's petrel had been named after one of my heroes, the artist-doctor Edward Wilson, who died in 1912 on the return journey of Scott's fateful expedition to the South Pole. He was a highly competent and humane naturalist, and although he collected specimens for the British Museum, he preferred to sketch the living bird in its environment. His pictures of this storm petrel of Antarctica are delightful, as reproduced in Dr Brian Roberts' edition of material from

Wilson's sketch-books, *Birds of the Antarctic*, published in 1967. However, the bird was first sketched by Sidney Parkinson in December 1768, from a specimen taken off the River Plate in the South Atlantic, during Captain James Cook's first voyage in the *Endeavour*. This bird is still in the British Museum (Natural History) collection; so far north in the breeding season it must have been an immature bird, born, as we now know, many hundreds of kilometres south. But if any thought had at that time been given to where the species nested, it would have been supposed that it was wintering in the South Atlantic, from breeding grounds believed to be in the northern hemisphere. For it was exceedingly numerous, and well known for centuries to fishermen and whalers sailing off the Newfoundland fishing banks during the northern summer. It was thought at that time to breed somewhere in the West Indies or Florida.

Dr Brian Roberts of the Scott Polar Research Institute details the further history of the common and scientific names in his monograph (1940) of the bird. It was actually named after one Alexander Wilson who in 1813 described it as virtually identical with the British storm petrel. In 1820 Heinrich Kuhl named it *Procellaria oceanica* from a specimen in the collection of Temminck; then, in honour of Alexander Wilson, another taxonomist in 1824 renamed the bird occurring in the North Atlantic *Procellaria wilsoni*. The famous artist Audubon in *Birds of America* (1840–44) seems to have confused its nesting ground with that of the

Great skuas attacking Wilson's storm petrel

Antarctic breeding ground of Wilson's storm petrel

Leach's storm petrel, believing that Wilson's must also nest on Canadian coasts, so numerous was it in the Gulf of St Lawrence in summer. He painted both, showing their distinct characters successfully, rear and front views. Not until the British Transit of Venus expedition in 1874 was the mystery of its breeding first discovered. Nests and eggs were found on the sub-Antarctic island of Kerguelen. But not until the era of Antarctic exploration opened with the turn of the century was the extent of its breeding grounds revealed. Today we know that it nests at points around the whole of the Antarctic continent and its nearer islands, including the islands of the Scotia Arc, and north to South Georgia, the Falkland Islands, and islands close to Cape Horn, also on Heard and Kerguelen Islands on the Indian Ocean side of Antarctica.

Brian Roberts was a young man when he took part in the British Graham Land Expedition of 1934–7. He told me he was determined to follow the same simple techniques I had used in studying storm petrels at Skokholm: a lattice of light material at the entrance to the burrows, as little handling as possible, use of a wire crook, etc, when he initiated his revealing study of a colony of Wilson's petrels on the Argentine Islands, which lie close under the long arm of the Antarctic Peninsula (Lat 65 15′S, Long 64 15′W).

It was on 7 February 1981 that, on board the *Lindblad Explorer*, with other naturalists, in perfect weather we passed south through the wondrously beautiful fiord of the Lemaire Channel, hardly half a kilometre wide, with stupendous snow-capped peaks rising into the clouds sheer from the sea. Small icebergs seemed to block our passage, but the ship weaved slowly through while we looked down on sleepy crab-eater seals and moulting Adélie penguins resting upon large ice floes and gazing back unafraid and quizzically at the admiring human figures lining the ship's rail. Now and then a giant petrel glided past with superb ease, in contrast with the heavy-winged Antarctic cormorant (also known as the blue-eyed shag *Phalacrocorax atriceps*), which lumbered along in whirring flight. As we emerged from Lemaire Strait there lay Peterman Island, where Charcot in 1908 wintered with his famous little exploration ship *Pourquoi Pas?*, and soon we saw the Argentine Islands where Brian Roberts conducted his study. The hardy little petrels were all about us in the swirling mixture of sea-ice and tide-rip, snatching up the abundant *Euphausia superba* shrimps. These they would digest for their own benefit, or semi-digest and feed to the newly hatched chicks in their burrows, as described by Roberts on those very islands ahead of us!

We had met Wilson's petrels at sea every day since leaving Tierra del Fuego on 1 February, and they remained the ship's Mother Carey companions all the way to Scott Base, and north again as far as the Balleny Islands, which we passed on 23 February. We examined their nesting grounds in the screes of Deception Island, and other islands southward through the Gerlache Strait, but having only a few hours ashore at each site, did not disturb their hidden homes deep under the stones. It was a good rule aboard the *Lindblad Explorer* that we were not to interfere in any way with breeding birds. Even to walk through a colony of nesting penguins invited predatory gull, skua, giant petrel or sheathbill to attack any undefended egg or small chick. Small birds such as storm petrel, prion and diving petrel depend for survival by day on remaining hidden and undisturbed in their burrows.

Next to study in the field and monograph Wilson's petrel after Brian Roberts were two scientists with the British Antarctic Survey, J. P. Beck and D. W. Brown (1972), during the summers of 1966 to 1969. Their study area was Factory Cove on Signy Island, South Orkney Islands, which lie farther north in the windy open sea (60 43′S, 45 38′W) and have become a main centre for biological research since 1962. Climatically, despite its lower latitude, Signy is as tough for the little bird as the Argentine Islands, as we shall see. About the same period, F. Lacan studied this petrel in a very different environment, in 1967–8, at the French research station at Terre Adélie on the mainland of Antarctica between 136 and 142 E.

From the results of these three expeditions the breeding biology of Wilson's petrel has been accurately worked out, showing only a few variations, which are evidently due to different climatic conditions. For example, although the minimum incubation period in all three proves to be virtually the same as for our British species—thirty-nine days—the fledging period at Terre Adélie was forty-eight days, at the Argentine Islands it was fifty-two, and on Signy Island sixty days. This indicates that overall breeding success was greatest nearer the pole, under somewhat longer midsummer sunlight, and probably with access to more abundant food supply. These could be the main factors—taking the most obvious view.

Courtship and Mating

Generally the adult breeder returns from its seven-month northwards voyage to its Antarctic home with the melting of the ice and snow which have covered its burrows all winter. First arrivals early in November do not land immediately, but hover above their snow-covered homes of last year, evidently locating and 'remembering', that is, refreshing their memory of the exact location. On wind-swept screes there may be no snow, but still they do not enter the crevice leading to the old nest. This circling reconnaissance has another purpose—of meeting a partner, which if he or she be still alive, will be last year's mate engaged in the same pursuit. They will without doubt recognise each other on the wing by voice, by the twittering sounds they utter as they circle above the familiar site.

As in so many birds, the male Wilson's storm petrel is the first to come to earth a few days after returning to the colony. He attends to the problem of cleaning snow from the entrance, and spring-cleaning the burrow inside. He calls to the female to join him, which she does within the next few nights. The procedure follows that of the mated Skokholm storm-petrel pair—night visits are obligatory. But the summer solstice is near, there is only twilight at midnight in November, and the sun will not set at all between late November and early January. Nevertheless, the majority of storm petrels come home from sea between 9 p.m. and 2 a.m. and leave again before 5 a.m., during the period when most of their gull, skua and other predators are asleep or resting.

Mating usually takes place inside the burrow. Roberts mentions a harsh chattering call which is repeated in the burrow during courtship, possibly while copulating (as in some gulls). The nest-sites easiest to observe on the Argentine Islands were in natural cavities beneath bright green moss hummocks; they averaged about 40cm long and opened into a small chamber containing the nest, a shallow depression in a collection of moss-root fragments. These burrows were found to be used year after year; new material being placed on the top of old containing the remains of shells from which chicks had hatched in previous summers. In one nest these shell remains indicated that in five past seasons eggs had successfully hatched. Nest-lining is haphazard, the adult bringing home any material handy;

scraps of moss in moss burrows, penguin feathers (which are very small and fine) near colonies where penguins moult; bits of paper and other human waste scraps near the Signy station. But in bare screes there is little or no lining; the egg is laid on whatever debris is present naturally, such as dust and disintegrated rock. In northerly colonies, in the Falklands and Cape Horn area, more substantial linings of stalks and dead leaves are brought in from the surrounding vegetation.

Desirable established burrows are hard to come by, and much competed for in some thickly inhabited Antarctic colonies; new ones may be excavated in unsuitable places. Edward Wilson describes a burrow at Cape Adare in which the floor of the tunnel was smooth ice, and the nest cavity lined with penguin feathers. In the South Orkneys Ardley (1936) excavated six burrows 'actually made in blocks of ice which had evidently formed among the rocks during the winter'.

The intensity of night visits by the mated pair reaches a climax about three weeks before the egg is laid. The bare brood patch in both sexes is fully developed during this courtship and mating period. Then, about ten days before she lays, the mated female departs and no longer pays visits to her mate at night. She remains feeding at sea to build up the developing egg. Her husband however comes home each night—a necessary visit in order to keep guard on the burrow which may be pirated by other adults seeking a home. Whether he repels intruders vigorously then is difficult to observe. Beck and Brown record that when fingers were inserted, in one burrow where this was possible, the bird in possession 'nibbled tentatively at the intruding fingers'; possibly, these observers think, any bird entering the dark hole may be treated at first by the occupant as if it was a returning mate, and its subsequent response to bill-nibbling, head-preening and voice determines what the occupant will do—spit oil if it disapproves of a stranger! They add: 'Repeated visits by one or more birds which have just attained sexual maturity, to an adult male which has lost its mate, may explain the few authenticated cases of replacement eggs recorded in storm petrels.'

Incubation

After her interval of building up condition, the female returns to lay the egg—the great occasion in the annual cycle of the mated pair. The egg is large for such a small bird—average measurements 34.8 × 24.7mm. It weighs 11g—the average mean adult weight is 38g. Like the British storm-petrel egg it is pure white, the big end zoned with faint reddish-brown and lilac spots. Its surprising size is evidently the result of being formed slowly over ten days' absence of the female, feeding upon the nourishing krill, which is extremely rich in protein and fat, essential for the development of fat reserves in an embryo which will be exposed to low and sometimes freezing temperatures during the forty days of incubation.

For the hazards of drifting snow are ever present, even in the summer days of December, when incubation normally begins. Thus 31 out of 82 eggs laid in two summers at Signy were affected by snow blockage denying the parents access to continue incubation. An unknown number of eggs were lost earlier in the same period when drift snow prevented some females from entering their burrows and laying their egg. Brave little petrel, that you should dare to nest in such inhospitable places! Roberts records how the devoted parents try successively but sometimes in vain to reach the entombed egg or chick: 'Footprints all round the blocked burrows indicated that on most of these occasions the parents had tried to reach home but failed. If the snow was soft they generally succeeded in burrowing through up to about 20cm, but deeper drifts kept them out.'

Forty days' incubation at least, so the egg will not hatch before mid or late February; and already, when we were leaving Antarctica on 23 February, winter was closing in. The penguins had finished nesting and were standing around looking fat but miserable in their autumn moult, willing to sail away on suitable ice floes but not yet ready to wet their mixture of old and new feathers. The 'summer scientists' at the several Antarctic research stations we had visited were already packed up to go, or had gone north, like migratory birds, leaving only a skeleton overwintering crew.

Snow does not fall heavily in Antarctica, but after the brief mid-summer melting period it ceases to thaw as the sun loses its strength. In the dry below-zero temperatures of late February onwards, strong winds cause drifts of surface snow which are often more dangerous to the burrow-nesting petrels. Also, as Roberts records, if a milder spell with rain occurs then, the subsequent frost draws a hard sheet of ice over the drifted snow; or if a wet fog intervenes there is a considerable development of rime, which will grow out as a wall of ice to windward, effectively blocking the nest-holes. Helpless to save them, Roberts watched parents on such occasions trying in vain to dig their way in, afterwards fluttering to and fro in distress. Should drift snow reach the unguarded egg, the embryo will die within hours.

Why should these feeble little birds nest in such a dangerous terrain and climate? You would suppose that, by the process of the survival of the fittest and the death of the failures, only suitable burrows safe from these hazards would be occupied. We may speculate that this would be the case in a diminishing population; but as this little bird is so visibly abundant everywhere close inshore around Antarctica in summer, there is evidently considerable pressure on the limited number of safe sites, as already mentioned, forcing new breeders to seek for and occupy places subject to greater snow and ice hazards.

Once the egg is laid, the male usually incubates for the first shift, while his wife recuperates at sea. But with food easily procured she may come back the next night, her hunger satisfied. There is evidently competition to incubate, resulting in short shifts of forty-eight hours each. But both seem to visit the nest each night, when pretty recognition ceremonies of bill-grasping and nibbling take place as the pair meet and chatter together over the egg. But there is no mating, and no exchange of food, just an excited renewal of the pair bond. The incoming bird is eager to incubate, and has been seen to scratch at its partner by raising one webbed foot, aggressively rather than fondly, in an attempt to obtain possession of the egg. Such eagerness is important, for it prevents the egg becoming chilled by the low temperature of the air in the burrow. Normally this does not fall below zero, Roberts found; during the early period of incubation, although the night air temperature outside fell below $0°C$, it was constant between $0°C$ and $5°C$ inside the nest cavity. Beck and Brown managed to test the actual temperature within the egg itself by sealing a thermistor probe within, which, during the nineteenth day of incubation, registered $36.8°C$. The normal average body temperature of the adult bird is $38.8°C$.

All being well, under regular and continuous incubation the egg hatches in thirty-eight to forty days. Any extra period is due to it being neglected for that number of days of temporary desertion. But there is a limit of neglect—measured by these observers as nine days left cold—beyond which the embryo dies.

The supreme moment of successful hatching requires steady incubation heat for several days beforehand and after. It is doubtless signalled, as described for our Skokholm petrel earlier, by the first tapping of the chick's egg-tooth against the shell as soon as it breaks the soft lining of the embryonic shroud, and air enters its lungs from the warm mini-atmosphere under the unbroken but porous shell of the big end. As soon as this happens the chick, still coiled in its cramped embryonic posture, begins its first feeble calls and efforts to emerge. But having cracked the shell at last, it will rest for several hours as it breathes the fresh oxygenated air of the burrow, before resuming the struggle beneath the warm brood patch. Picture, if we may, the joy of the proud parent as, moving a little restlessly in that chill dark nursery above the permafrost of the Antarctic subsoil or rock scree, to accommodate the movements of the life it must continue to keep warm, it bends its head to fondle and assist as best it may the squeaking child in its discomfort and damp struggle to emerge.

The Nestling

February is the main month of hatching, with very few chicks born in the last days of January. Complete emergence, from the moment the egg is chipped, takes twenty-four to forty-eight hours. The chick dries out under the warm parental brood patch, and proves to be well covered with a dark grey down. Unlike the British storm petrel, the Wilson's chick does not develop a second down; the first suffices, growing a little more fluffy during the first week or so. There is no down on the facial area, which remains bare until the first juvenile feathers appear about the thirtieth day.

Birth weight averages, when dry, just over 7g, steadily increasing in healthy well-fed chicks to ten times that weight, before reducing a little (having become too fat) before departure from the nest, when the mean weight of fledgelings at Signy and the Argentine Islands was just under 60g. The nestling is born blind, its eyelids closed as if glued together, but they open about the tenth day; the legs darken at seven to ten days, when the wing-quills begin to sprout and the egg-tooth falls off. As the body feathers develop the down thins and gradually drops away, but a little still clings to the fully feathered child at fifty days. Minimum fledging period is fifty-two days, which means that the chick departs normally during late March; but those born late, and chicks which have suffered periods of starvation from snow blockage or other accidents, may not leave until winter is well advanced in April.

These studies found that the male parent in the marked nests attended the young chick more often than the female; although it is not clear why. For the first two to five days the chick was brooded, and needed to be kept warm, continuously, but afterwards, having achieved a natural homoiothermic state (of balanced temperature with control of heat production and loss), it was left alone by day. It was refuelled on almost each night for the first three weeks, by one or both parents. Roberts considered that there was no real desertion of the few chicks which reached fledging stage in his marked burrows; he notes that 'The burrow is sometimes visited for several nights *after* the chick has flown, but it was not possible to determine whether these visits were made by the chicks or the adults'. But Beck and Brown found that, during the last ten days, feeding of the chicks became more sporadic, ending in a short period of starvation of from three to five days immediately prior to departure. The successful fledgelings were fatter by about 45 per cent above adult weight, and therefore in no hurry to feed when they reached the sea; they were in better condition in fact than our Skokholm petrel whose fledgelings leave when about 20 per cent above adult weight.

Departure Flight

By the time the fledgeling is ready to fly in April and early May the nights are longer than the days. Already in the last ten days the nestling has become active enough to move freely along the burrow, and a few venture outside to exercise their wings before taking off. Those which stay in daylight outside the burrow for any length of time, however, are at risk from scavenging kelp gulls (*Larus dominicanus*), skuas, giant petrels and sheath-bills, still present though in smaller numbers in this autumn season. Fresh winds may assist the fledgeling to take off, but gales sometimes blow it inland or cause it to strike some object such as a cliff or ice wall. Any weakness of flight or resting on the ground resulting from this misfortune is almost instantly spotted by the first aerial predator, which will swoop and devour the petrel.

Survival rates at fledging time from all causes, including some unavoidable disturbances by inquisitive scientists, were very low in these studies. Of twenty chicks under observation at Galindez Island in 1935 only seven survived to leave the burrow—a mortality of 65 per cent. On Signy in 1966–7, twenty-two eggs in marked nests hatched and sixteen chicks successfully fledged; in 1967–8, three eggs hatched but no chicks fledged; in the next summer at least ten eggs hatched but no chicks fledged—a dismal average of 11 per cent breeding success rate over the three years, representing a mortality of 89 per cent. This is a quite insupportable loss at so tender an age, which Beck and Brown attribute to exceptional bad weather and snow-blockage. However, the same authors calculate from measurements of ice-free areas, with suitable nesting habitat, and from results of mist-netting counts, that the total population of Wilson's petrel on Signy Island at this time was about 200,000 pairs, of which they considered that about one-half must be young pre-breeders. (For discussion of longevity and age composition in storm-petrel species, see page 93.)

The Adolescents

We have shown that a mist-netting programme is invaluable in estimating the proportion of breeding adults to non-breeding visitors, and to check the movements of failed breeders within a given study area. The results of the marking of thousands of British storm petrels have been described earlier. But until we have the results of recent banding of large numbers of Wilson's petrels, we can only quote the mean adult survival estimates of those banded in 1959–62 by Beck and Brown (1972). By extrapolation of all data available at that time, they arrive at a figure of 90.83 per cent, a mean annual adult mortality of 9.175. From these estimates they judge that mean adult life

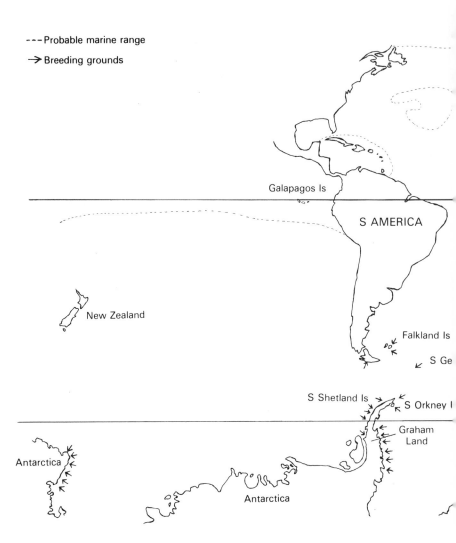

--- Probable marine range

→ Breeding grounds

Galapagos Is

S AMERICA

New Zealand

Falkland Is

S Ge

S Shetland Is

S Orkney I

Graham Land

Antarctica

Antarctica

expectancy is 10.4 years. If so, our fledgeling Wilson's petrel has an average of 10.4 years in which to find and win a mate, and reproduce itself sufficiently to provide heirs to carry on the species at its present high level of numbers. But first it must spend, we believe from the example of the immature British storm petrel, a few years wandering the oceans within its wide range of sea-room, before that serious business of marriage becomes pressing.

Not to labour the point we have already made in describing the footloose and wingfree wanderings of the adolescent British storm petrels, as proved by mist-netting thousands, we can picture with confidence the fledgeling Wilson's petrel's northward flight to escape the chill gloom, snowstorms, ice and darkness of Antarctic seas. But as it seems much more gregarious as well as more numerous at sea than our Skokholm bird, and some adults (though

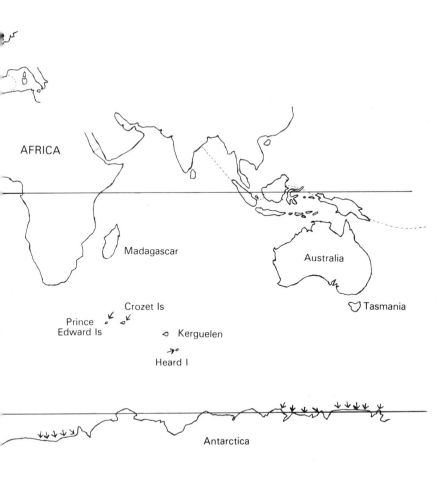

AFRICA

Madagascar

Australia

Crozet Is

Prince
Edward Is

Kerguelen

Heard I

Tasmania

Antarctica

Breeding grounds and marine range of Wilson's storm petrel

they may be virgins) visit the breeding burrows after the fledgelings have departed, these youngsters may soon meet and mingle freely with the north-bound older adults and adolescent visitors. Brian Roberts in his monograph produces twelve chart-maps of the month-by-month migration of Wilson's petrel between Antarctica and the limits of its northern range in the Atlantic, just short of the Arctic Circle. Each dot is a sight record. The main movement north begins in March away from the normal summer feeding and breeding latitude around Cape Horn, the Falklands, South Georgia and southwards. During April the birds are already recorded along the whole of the eastern seaboard of South and North America, north to Long Island; also off South Africa and north across the equator to Cape Verde. In May and June huge flocks are concentrated on the turbulent fishing grounds south of the Canadian coast, close to the New England

shore; while a smaller migration has moved north from West Africa to
Moroccan and Iberian coasts—a few enter the Mediterranean. During the
northern midsummer flocks are feeding in the Gulf Stream or North
Atlantic Drift current right across the Atlantic from Newfoundland to the
south-west approaches of the British Isles, reached in July and August.

The southward migration begins in September; comparatively few—
probably all non-breeders—are left along the east coast of North America,
but there are numerous records in this month indicating a migration from
the Bay of Biscay, following the easterly trade winds through the Canary and
Cape Verde Isles, and diagonally south-south-west across the equator
during October to the coast of Brazil. Very few adults are reported north of
the equator during the northern winter. The majority have executed a
circling annual flight of the Atlantic Ocean typical of some other long-
distance travellers (eg great and Manx shearwaters, Arctic tern) which make
use of trade winds.

Migration in the Indian Ocean is also a well-marked circle, but
constricted by the northern land barriers of India, Arabia and East Africa.
In the southern Pacific Wilson's petrel is thinly distributed, but not
infrequently seen in the cold Humboldt Current as far north as Peru; but
farther north in the tropical convergence there are so many resident and
visiting storm petrel species that accurate sight identification is not easy.

As long ago as 1936 Murphy expressed the belief that the 'juvenal' birds
spent their first year entirely at sea, from finding that so many Wilson's
petrels taken off the tropical coasts of South America and Africa (usually
close to the land) were in unmoulted juvenile plumage. They behaved in a
leisurely manner, frequently resting in rafts on the water, 'a custom
apparently not characteristic of adult birds'. Adults keep farther at sea,
hurrying on tireless wings to reach the cool upwelling waters of northern
fishing banks. Like the British storm petrel, Wilson's will follow summer all
its life, leaving the northern autumn to discover the southern summer has
arrived at its well-remembered Antarctic homes.

Moult

Complete moult of the adult plumage takes place from May to August
during the sojourn in the North Atlantic and South Pacific. In the Indian
Ocean this adult moult is apparently delayed until July—from examination
of birds taken in that tropical 'wintering' area. The juvenile, arriving later
and remaining in the tropical seas, has no occasion to lose its first waterproof
suit for a year, and retains it until after the adults have passed south through
the tropics again. Like the juvenile British storm petrel, it is happy to linger
in the warm seas, beginning its first complete moult while its parents are

away breeding. When they return north in the following May the young bird will be about seventeen months old and in its new plumage; and as an adolescent may join the adults at least for part if not all of their circling migration. Meanwhile their younger (three or four months old) brothers and sisters will have moved in turn to winter in the same traditional tropical or sub-tropical latitudes.

Return of the pre-breeders

Banding of Wilson's nestlings may one day prove that the first return to the home breeding grounds will not be until the individual is at least two years old, that it will not necessarily land then, but will flit about above several colonies, looking for a future home and mate. In its third summer it will form an attachment to one site by landing and inspection, but unless it is early made the partner of a bereaved adult, it will not mate and breed successfully. Not until it is four or five years old will it settle down to a successful partnership in one burrow, which, if it proves suitable for the task, the pair will use for the rest of their lives.

Graceful (or Elliot's) Storm Petrel *Oceanites gracilis*

This is a miniature Wilson's petrel, perhaps derived from the Antarctic or southernmost Chilean stock of *O. oceanicus*. Possibly, long ago, some individuals during the early non-breeding period of their young lives migrated north along the Humboldt Current, and on reaching the Galapagos Islands settled to breed there, and never returned south. In doing so, they became the next-to-smallest of the storm petrels, very dark, and quite distinct by the white of the rump extending in a band under the tail. Averaging only 148mm in length, the graceful storm petrel is just two or three millimetres longer than the least petrel (page 179). Like Wilson's, it has very long legs, with a yellow middle to the webs.

The graceful storm petrel is a true species, separated from Wilson's by several characters. It conforms to Bergmann's Rule that the body size of closely related species and subspecies increases with decreasing mean temperature of its habitat. Some separatists have placed the large breeding birds of Antarctica in a separate subspecies *exasperatus*, reserving the trinomial *O. o. oceanicus* for those breeding on Chilean and sub-Antarctic islands, which are statistically smaller. We note these interesting subspecific differences: they are, in simple terms, the result of environmental influences. Very remarkably no nest of *O. gracilis* (also known as Elliot's storm petrel) has ever been found, even by students of the storm petrels breeding in the Galapagos (Harris, 1969). But it is commonly seen close inshore there, and has been sighted off the coast of Peru and south to Chile.

Various authors have wondered about the significance of the yellow webs in both *Oceanites* and the white-faced storm petrel *Pelagodroma marina* (next chapter). But unless one is within a few metres of these petrels in flight, the yellow panels are not conspicuous to the human eye. Zinc and Eldridge (1981) suggest what is extremely difficult to prove, that 'It is possible that the yellow webs, when dangled in the water, serve either to lure krill (by eliciting a swarming reaction) or to frighten them, in either instance making them more conspicuous to the petrel. Wilson's petrels also eat squid (*Decapoda*), which prey on krill. It is possible, therefore, that the petrel attracts the squid by mimicking the krill, and then eats the squid.' Other birds stir the water to draw their live prey into view, notably herons and some waders. The sea-going phalaropes spin rapidly as they swim at the surface, then snap up planktonic food swirling around them. Cape pigeons, *Daption capensis*, swim forward, deliberately paddling their feet to draw krill towards the thrusting bill, which scoops the food up and strains away the water through the serrations at the side of the bill.

Watching Wilson's petrels feeding at sea, our impression has been that they do not so much dangle their yellow webbed feet in the water as use them to prevent submergence, as far as possible, as that might have a

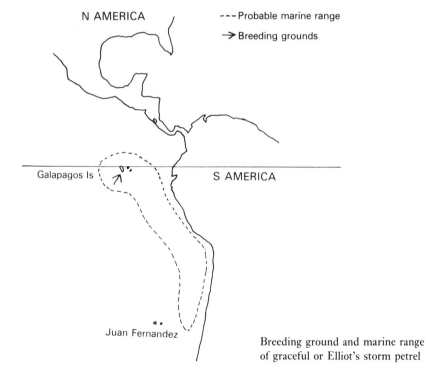

Breeding ground and marine range of graceful or Elliot's storm petrel

Graceful or Elliot's storm petrels

capsizing or tripping effect. We have never seen any petrel deliberately hover and 'mark time' with its paddles churning the water in one spot. It will occasionally dive briefly, quickly emerging in flight within a second or two, dry-winged. Normally Wilson's, like the British storm petrel, skips about rapidly and erratically, with short swinging glides, using its feet, with the webs spread, to bounce off the surface each time it dips its head to seize a food item.

The significance of yellow panels in the webs remains a mystery; at least as much as the yellow of the legs and feet of certain diurnal wading birds and cormorants, which are brightest during prenuptial courtship. But Wilson's petrel courts, displays and mates in the darkness of its burrow.

Dangers at Sea

All storm petrels are exposed to these, although it seems to be comparatively rare for Wilson's petrel to be wrecked in large numbers on the shore after a great gale. Perhaps it is better equipped than most petrels to withstand storms, beginning with the savage chill Antarctic autumn winds when it leaves home for the first time.

Seals, sea-lions and leopard seals take penguins freely, but they may find it less easy to snatch up storm petrels, even when these are feeding on the blood, oil and scraps of flesh from their larger prey. But, as already

Peregrine falcon with prey—a frigate or white-faced storm petrel

mentioned, in handling storm petrels for ringing we and other observers occasionally notice a leg missing or mutilated, the stump healed, and there is sometimes injury to the webbing of the toes, indicating attacks from below, some probably by large fish. Healthy storm petrels are nimble enough on the wing to escape the swoop of predatory skuas and other large birds at sea, and are usually immune from—or evade—attack from such birds encountered at a source of food of mutual interest, such as swarming fish or the carcases of animals.

Unusual records of casualties at sea have occurred when small gulls and petrels have hovered over and fed from a turbulent mass of krill rounded up and forced to the surface by feeding whales (as we have seen in Alaskan waters). Occasionally, when the whale sucks the huge ball of plankton and water into its enormous gape and stomach, the hovering birds sink with the whirlpool. This has given rise to the erroneous statement in some books that the humpback whale includes sea birds in its regular diet.

During their migrations, peregrine and other falcons which feed on flying birds frequently settle on the mast or yard of a ship at sea; from this artificial lookout they will strike and kill small birds, including storm petrels, fluttering and feeding in the ship's wake.

Southern storm petrels

We have already mentioned the excitement of finding tens of thousands of yet another storm petrel new to us, in the wild and beautiful environment of a warm night upon a sub-tropical island far in the open ocean. And one so elegant, pale-coloured and fairylike in flight, so gentle in behaviour when picked up, that the little black, white-rumped storm petrels described earlier seem by comparison querulous gnomes and black goblins!

The Frigate or White-faced Storm Petrel *Pelagodroma marina*

It was just after midnight, about 1.30 a.m. on 16 July 1939 that we first met the frigate or white-faced storm petrel, as we climbed the steep path from the dark landing ravine of Grande Selvagen, which lies about 290km south of Madeira in the open Atlantic. There were great numbers in the air,

Frigate or white-faced storm petrel

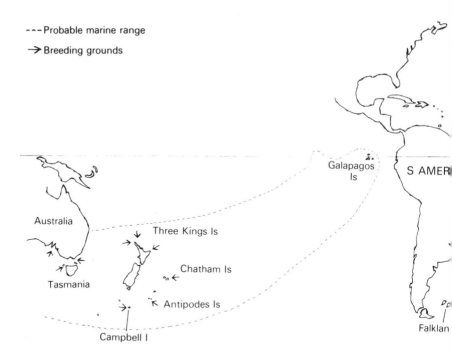

Australia

Three Kings Is

Chatham Is

Tasmania

Antipodes Is

Campbell I

Galapagos Is

S AMER

Falklan

revealed in our torchbeam as hovering, dancing white forms, long legs dangling as if ready, but hesitant, to alight. Possibly they were uttering faint calls, but if so their voices were unheard in the positive roar of wailing and barking noises from equally numerous and much larger nesting and flighting Atlantic great shearwaters and Bulwer's petrels (see page 116).

It was easy to take one in the hand when, dazzled by the light of the torch, it sat quietly on the bare ground, making no attempt to bite or struggle free. Thus held, the frigate petrel, its folded wings extending far beyond its tail, seems a good deal larger than Leach's or Wilson's petrels, but in fact it averages, at 20cm (8in), only 1cm more body length. The very long, yellow-webbed legs, extending well beyond the tail in flight, help this impression of greater size. It is wholly white underneath, the upper parts a delicate grey-brown, the square-cut tail black, rump and shoulders grey, the flight feathers brown. The face is handsomely set off by white brows and chin enclosing the extensive dark patch below the eye; the bill is black, the iris brown. The pale plumage pattern and the distinctive flight, hesitant and fluttering, make identification easy. As seen at sea when feeding, this storm petrel sometimes dips its long legs in the water, as well as using them to 'bounce', but without the forward walking progress of some storm petrels.

One estimate of their numbers on Grande Selvagen was a speculative guess of 100,000, but a 1963 estimate suggests the real figure is around half a million. The plateau which extends over most of the top of this island was

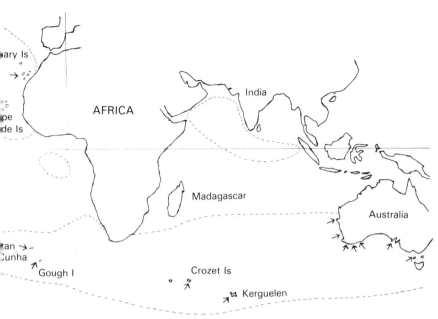

Breeding grounds and marine range of frigate or white-faced storm petrel

covered with a phosphatic soil in which, as already described, three small petrel species were nesting, to some extent avoiding competition for small burrow sites by dividing the year into separate breeding seasons. At that moment in July most of the burrows we opened—including those accidentally exposed by our feet breaking through—contained full-grown fat frigate-petrel fledgelings about to go to sea. Many of these still had tufts of their natal down adhering here and there.

During the day those fledgelings exposed by the guano-digging operations of Madeiran labourers, who were spending the summer there sacking the rich soil for export, were thrown to a posse of yellow-legged herring gulls, waiting expectantly nearby; but a few crawled in the hot sun to reach cover in an undisturbed burrow. These unfortunates uttered a faint protesting chittering squeak when picked up; but at this season at least, the adults that flew in on our second night seemed silent. The only adult note we recorded was very faint, and described in our diary as not unlike that of a redshank *Totanus totanus* heard at some distance. Observers elsewhere, less troubled perhaps by the louder songs of other petrels, have recorded a variety of frigate-petrel calls, all low-keyed and chiefly uttered from the burrow. L. E. Richdale, who studied a large colony of these (which he prefers to call white-faced) petrels on Whero, a rocky island of less than an acre off Stewart Island, New Zealand, considered there was considerable aerial calling above this small islet, but again there were three other petrels occupying burrows there. He was surprised to find that about half the total of frigate petrels visiting the burrows were non-breeders.

The apparent feebleness of this storm petrel on land, as we have studied it briefly at night on Grande Selvagen, on Fisher Island in the Bass Strait and on islets off New Zealand, hardly fits in with the fact of its abundance throughout its considerable world ocean range. We have found it the easiest of all storm petrels to catch by hand at night. On Grande Selvagen we caught several which had become momentarily entangled in the tall wands of *Nicotiana glauca* when rising in flight from their burrows. David Bannerman (1959) remarks that 'It is very sad that in its breeding places in the Cape Verde Islands and in the Selvagens this most attractive species is subject to so much persecution—mice, cats and crabs—for its colonies in the Atlantic islands are as nothing when we compare the numbers of individual birds with the enormous numbers which breed in the Australian and New Zealand seas.'

Tuatara or dragon lizard

True, it is a southern oceans' species; and like any other storm petrel, cannot survive on the small islands it inhabits in the permanent presence of introduced cats or rats. But it has long been able to survive and thrive despite some endemic predators such as gulls and land crabs; and in Australia the venomous tiger snake commonly inhabits burrows on several islands where *P. marina* nests. D. L. Serventy took me to some of those in the Bass Strait to band frigate petrels; the essential equipment for extracting them from holes was a thick leather gauntlet to protect the arm holding the wire crook! Large tiger snakes will devour some adult and young petrels, but not enough to cause serious depopulation. In the same way the unique tuatara or primitive dragon lizard *Sphenodon punctatus*, which shelters and co-exists in some burrows dug by diving and frigate storm petrels on a few New Zealand islands (where there are no cat or rat predators), is said to devour a petrel egg or chick occasionally.

It was while I was staying with Dom Serventy on the little 2 acre

Fisher Island, close to Flinders Island, that on the last night of November 1974, after checking on the banded individuals of the Tasmanian shearwater *Puffinus tenuirostris* colony (some 70 pairs) which he has been studying since 1947, we found a new colony of frigate storm petrels. Dom makes two or three visits to this tiny granitic islet each summer, timed to check the punctual arrival of the male shearwaters which come home from winter wandering (they travel by an astonishing figure-of-eight migration right across the Pacific to the Bering Sea and Arctic Ocean) before the females; then to check the arrival of the latter for mating and egg-laying; and in late summer he camps in his one-roomed hut there and bands the young birds and any visiting non-breeders.

These shearwaters are quite large (38cm from bill to tail) and excavate roomy burrows in the only suitably deep pocket of soil, which (like the Selvagens) has much drought-resistant *Mesembryanthemum* (iceplant) growing on the barer ground, but as the island has a damper, cooler climate it also supports some small low shrubs of *Olearia* and *Coprosma*. Evidently Dom had overlooked the presence of the storm petrels because, unlike storm petrels at Skokholm which will dig side burrows within the larger burrow of Manx shearwaters, these small *Pelagodroma* petrels had kept well clear of the Fisher Island shearwater burrows, and established themselves in shallow soil close to the edge of the sea. It was easy to overlook the entrances to their small burrows, overhung with grass and other low vegetation new-grown on top of many years' older growth.

But once we had spotted one storm petrel entering a hole that night, in the light of our torch, we explored the area thoroughly, and traced at least fifty occupied holes. Like pale fireflies they were coming in and departing throughout the dark hours. From some burrows we hooked out courting pairs and in two there was a single egg. It was clearly the beginning of the nesting season, as it was for Dom's beloved short-tailed shearwaters. Dom was wildly excited and called up friends on nearby Flinders Island on his walkie-talkie with 'the startling news'; he ordered leg-bands of suitably small size to begin a marking study of *Pelagodroma*. He insisted that the colonisation was very recent, otherwise he would have noticed it earlier.

Tiger snakes, which can swim, rarely cross to Fisher Island; to that extent the new colony of storm petrels would be safer here. And with the pleasing prospect of starting up another genealogical record, of generations of marked storm petrels, Dom invited his young aide, Nigel Brothers, nineteen years old (seconded to help Dom by the Tasmanian National Parks and Wildlife Service) to undertake the study.

'You're young enough to outlive me and the oldest storm petrel on Fisher,' he told him, as we three men fortified ourselves over coffee in the little hut. Dawn was breaking. Three of the large scarce Cape Barren Geese were arriving for their usual morning grazing session and to sleep on a nearby reef. Naturally I felt much at home on this beautiful little island so like Skokholm on a small scale, with nesting shearwater and storm petrel; even some of the wild flowers were the same, such as the sea tree-mallow *Lavatera*, and common cat's-ear *Hypochaeris*. Dom Serventy had modelled his shearwater study (he said) on our Skokholm one, beginning twenty years later, but keeping it intact to date. Checking on his card index the Fisher Island breeding shearwaters which we had recovered alive that day, he reported that one was his oldest *Puffinus tenuirostris*, a female of thirty years, allowing four years for adolescence before settling to breed in the marked burrows. (Our own sequence of marked Manx shearwaters, begun at Skokholm in 1929, could not match that longevity—it was broken by the war years 1940–45.)

World-wide, the score of storm petrel species we describe in this book have linked the marine ornithologists, who observe them at sea and on small islands, in a pleasant sharing of knowledge of their romantic lives, and speculation on the fascinating mysteries still unsolved. On that tiny Fisher Island it seemed almost as if the charming frigate petrels had deliberately settled in that year of 1974 to celebrate the reunion of Serventy and Lockley (for Dom had been to Skokholm earlier), both now of respectable longevity—the biblical allotted span . . . or thus we mused, discussing the island-going lives of these smallest oceanic birds.

Why, for instance, does this southern-ocean frigate storm petrel nest, aberrantly, on the Cape Verde Islands and the Selvagens, north of the equator? Its nearest breeding islands in the Atlantic are about 8,000km south in the Tristan da Cuhna group. Elsewhere it nests only off Australia and New Zealand. The only reasonable explanation seems to be that young unattached individuals, on their wandering adolescent migrations, have explored far and wide, sometimes perhaps blown in a small group far beyond their normal sea range. They have become lost, but remained sufficiently cohesive as a potential breeding unit to establish a new dynasty where conditions of food supply and isolation from predators on a small island encourage such settlement (see *Oceanites gracilis*, page 151).

'Hydrobatids—ugly collective scientific name for storm petrel species,' pontificated Dom, comfortably wedged in his chair at the table littered with his shearwater record sheets, 'seem to share the world's oceans in a pattern which reflects the seasonal abundance of their planktonic type of food, and the need to occupy the very limited breeding areas on small islands sufficiently free of predators to enable them to reproduce successfully.'

Their established migration routes are followed instinctively, that is to say they are genetically determined—or so most observers believe. But this theory does not explain why, during several years of adolescence, the immatures do not necessarily keep to the traditional ocean flyway of their parents, but wander circuitously for hundreds of miles off course; and when they do first approach their island birthplace, they may not land. Many will instead pay visits to, and even a year or so later settle to breed upon, another island.

Rather scornfully, in pleasant six o'clock supper sessions, before the main work of nocturnal observation began, we criticised the modern habit of some younger scientists who, in learned papers, try to explain these mysteries of migration, adaptive radiation, colonisation, and territory sharing ('limitation of numbers by space occupancy') in the new involved language of ecology and ethology, using words of many syllables. Such jargon (we said) produced ambiguities worse than the problems discussed. 'All we really know is that human behaviour achieves adaptiveness for survival by being intelligent, but animal behaviour achieves adaptiveness and survives by being instinctive; yet man and birds both learn from experience how to survive . . .'

'Words, words, words—it's the facts that really matter,' Dom warned and instructed young Nigel five days later, when we left him in charge for a few days while we explored other islands in the Bass Strait—a customary round which Dom makes while awaiting the return of the female shearwaters to lay their single egg in his marked burrows on Fisher Island. In another five days we returned home (as Dom loved to call his summertime island paradise) towards dusk to find Nigel had a number of satisfactory facts to present to us. He had not been idle. First, he had repainted Dom's shack a pleasant green to match its background of greenery and lichened granite rocks. Secondly, he had cooked a splendid welcome-home supper, of abalone and crayfish, freshly collected over the low spring tide. And thirdly, he was rightly proud of having twenty-five burrows of storm petrels actively occupied by mated pairs, and more females laying their egg. Obeying Dom's instructions he had marked every burrow with a stick on which was painted in red its identification number. There had only been one casualty: one of the newly ringed occupants had blundered against the fresh paint on the stick beside its burrow before the paint had dried, and so light is this little petrel that it had failed to struggle free and had died before Nigel could rescue it on his dawn round of inspection. Otherwise the new banding study was successfully launched. Just a few pairs seemed to have abandoned some of the total of fifty burrows originally discovered; this one can put down partly to human interference in the private lives of these little birds, as we had found at Skokholm.

Breeding and Social Behaviour

From such continuing and past studies, particularly by L. E. Richdale on Whero Island, and John Warham in both Australia and New Zealand, the social and breeding biology of *Pelagodroma marina* has been fairly well elucidated; and as expected closely resembles that of most other members of the Hydrobatid family. (We might note, in passing, that the English names of white-faced and frigate storm petrel are unsatisfactory, and confuse the beginner, since there are also white-bellied and black-bellied species of storm petrel, scientifically of the *Fregetta* genus; and as described later in this chapter, there is also the white-throated storm petrel, *Nesofregetta*, perhaps fortunately confined to the tropical western and central Pacific, away from the range of our *P. marina*, which it resembles at a distance.

Our *P. marina* is abundant off the south and west coasts of Australia, and all three main islands of New Zealand. Here, as at Tristan da Cuhna, it is a summer nester, arriving in October, and laying the single egg during November in shallow burrows which it is capable of digging if necessary. The egg, white with the usual red-brown ring of fine spots, averages 36 × 27mm, weight 14g. Incubation is shared in shifts of two to five days, occasionally longer. It takes longer, fifty-five to fifty-six days, to hatch than any other storm petrel so far adequately studied, but probably as a result the new-born nestling has its eyes open and is very active by comparison. This precocity is evidently also one reason why it is not continuously brooded for more than the first two to four days, although fed by one or both parents each night for about the first fortnight. Meals then become fewer but larger. There is one down only, a pale mouse-grey, the chin and crown bare but soon concealed by the rapidly grown fluffy down of the nape. At five weeks the nestling weighs about 65g, and as the feathers develop the young bird continues to put on weight up to a maximum of just over 100g. During the

Fledgeling frigate or white-faced storm petrel

The handsome frigate or white-faced storm petrel

week before departure from the burrow, when fifty-two to sixty-seven days old, it loses weight rapidly. Although some adults may continue to visit the vacated burrow, at night only, Richdale was in doubt about their identity; they could well have been 'idle unringed' visiting storm petrels, a category which in numbers seemed to be as plentiful as the established breeding stock under study at Whero Rock. The rapid reduction in weight of the fledgeling in the week before departure indicated that it had not been fed and was, by losing its baby fat, preparing for the formidable occasion of launching into the darkness of night and sea for the first time.

This is the most vulnerable moment of the storm petrel's life, as described for other species in this book. On the small rocky islets of the Noisies of the Hauraki Gulf, which I can see from the window of my New Zealand home, the small colonies of white-faced storm petrels breeding there suffer only minor predation from a few resident large *Larus dominicanus* gulls; most of the fledgelings seem able to reach the sea safely, so close to their natal burrows. (When brown rats, *Rattus norvegicus*, reached one of these islets, they quickly exterminated the storm petrels, but a few years later the rats starved to death, and now the storm petrels are returning to nest once more.)

Describing to us his visit in 1982 to South-east Island in the Chathams, to study the ecology of the great skua *Catharacta lonnbergi*, our friend Professor E. C. Young reported that this 216 hectare sanctuary continues to support several hundred thousand (possibly a million) breeding white-faced storm petrels. (With no mammalian predators, it is the home of a plover and snipe found nowhere else.) On a summer night these petrels descend like a blizzard upon you, making it hard to walk, or even to see other birds. They crash-land through the low bush, and scuttle off to their holes in the soft earth. The skuas—about 100 pairs—fill up nightly on them, swallow them whole, and later, at their roosting place, regurgitate the bones and feathers in a neat pellet. Of course this annual predation of a few thousand storm petrels is almost without significance in such a huge petrel population. Not only can they take it, but the fighting for nesting burrows that seems to go on indicates that this little bird is highly successful. Good luck to you, handsome, gentle *Pelagodroma marina*, for you will need it in a world where pressures of human overpopulation, and the predatory animals man introduces everywhere he settles, have already destroyed so many of your former breeding colonies.

Black-bellied Storm Petrel *Fregetta tropica*

This and the next species, the white-bellied storm petrel, are difficult to separate at sea. Both are the same size, about 20cm, square-tailed and white under the wing, and the black line from the black throat down the centre of the white belly in *F. tropica* is often not only hard to see, but occasionally missing, as observed from a ship at sea; they will follow a ship freely, to pick up food churned up in the wake.

Black-bellied storm petrels

Dove prions

F. tropica is a misnomer, since the black-bellied species breeds only on sub-Antarctic islands: South Georgia, South Orkneys, South Shetlands, Bouvet, Crozet, Kerguelen, Auckland, Bounty (probably) and Antipodes Islands. It has been studied by Beck & Brown (1971) on the South Orkney Islands, and by Turner at South Georgia. Here it shares the rocky terrain and the hazard of snow-blocked burrows with Wilson's petrel. But it is much less numerous on, and at sea near, those breeding grounds.

In fact it is something of a mystery how two species so alike in size and food requirements can co-exist in the same breeding and feeding grounds. Beck & Brown discuss this in their study at Signy Island, South Orkneys, over three seasons between December 1966 and April 1969. They found the most striking feature in the biology of *F. tropica* was the scarcity of the species, an unusual situation in Antarctic birds. Although well dispersed over the whole coastal area free of permanent ice and snow, the total population on Signy was estimated at not more than 200 pairs; in the same zone an estimated 200,000 pairs of Wilson's storm petrels were nesting, and 50,000 dove prions *Pachyptila desolata*.

The prion is too large (27cm) to compete for the small nest-crevices used by the two storm petrels. Although Wilson's petrel arrives a little earlier at Signy than the black-bellied storm petrel, Beck & Brown could find no evidence of competition between them for the same nest sites—deep in talus slopes of small and large stones and boulders. In both species untimely late snow might delay the moment of egg-laying, or entomb the occupant.

We do not know the black-bellied storm petrel, beyond having seen it rarely at sea near the South Shetland Islands, where it nests in similar talus slopes with Wilson's. Both are strictly nocturnal; but at midsummer in the Antarctic and sub-Antarctic islands it is light enough to see the storm petrels when they fly home or conduct aerial displays between 10 p.m. and 2 a.m. in December and January. Brown saw black-bellied storm petrels displaying on 28 January 1969 at Deception Island, South Shetlands; pairs of the birds 'after gaining height, glided downward in unison, with one bird maintaining position just above and behind the other. The "oystercatcher call" was heard—a sequence of PEE-EEP notes—but only from birds displaying in the air.'

Interestingly, on 5 February 1981, during a day visit from the *Lindblad Explorer* to this remarkable island, which is the mountainous rim of a sunken and still thermally active volcanic caldera, we climbed partway up those same Cathedral Crags in search of storm petrels. Plenty of Wilson's were making their grating chirps in the larva screes, and we heard the very different call of the black-bellied storm petrel several times from deep in the crevices between larger stones. This is a high-pitched whistling hum, aptly described by Beck and Brown as 'hüüüüü, lasting about four seconds and reminiscent of the flight call of a golden plover *Pluvialis apricaria*'. It is only uttered at the nest or near it. Unfortunately the heights were swathed in mist, the weather gradually deteriorated, and a strong wind made our ship's

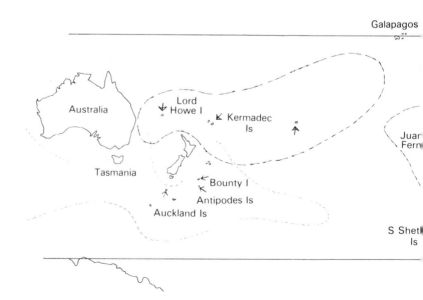

Breeding grounds and marine ranges of black-bellied and white-bellied storm petrels

continued anchorage inside the crater at risk. Our observations were cut short when, early in the afternoon, we were recalled (and thereby further denied the unusual luxury of a planned bathe in the hot springs issuing from fumaroles at Pendulum Cove). We did not see, only heard, storm petrels on Deception Island; but that evening at sea, in the open Bransfield Channel, we saw a few black-bellied storm petrels close to the ship, among hundreds of Wilson's. Apart from the white lower breast, which is swayed into view as the petrel flies with a distinctive banking movement, it does not patter on the water like Leach's or the British storm petrels, instead skipping over the surface with wings spread almost horizontally.

Arriving in November at Signy Island, *F. tropica* seeks rather more stable areas of consolidated scree, 'composed of small boulders approximately 20cm in diameter', recognisable to the human eye by the growth of several years of *Usnea* lichens. The male is present more often than the female before she lays her egg, which is typically white with a wreath of fine reddish spots. Size 37 × 27mm, mean weight 15g. As the average weight of fifteen females was 56.5g, the new-laid egg represents 26.5 per cent of the female body-weight. This percentage is close to that of the Wilson's storm petrels nesting next door (studied by the same observers at Signy), with egg weight 11g and adult body-weight 38.2g—percentage 28.5.

Pre-egg visits to the nest can last three weeks for the male *F. tropica* who,

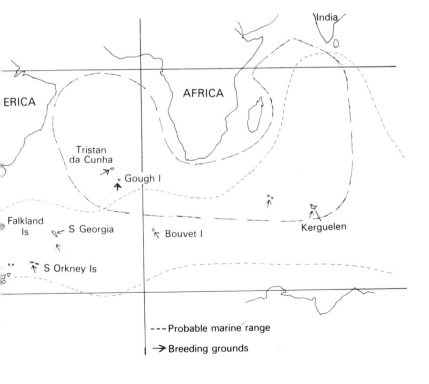

--- Probable marine range

→ Breeding grounds

as in other species, needs to guard the nest from home-seeking rivals. But the female, having mated, leaves at least a week earlier in order to feed and build up her egg at sea. The brood patches meanwhile develop by defeathering, and as soon as the egg is laid the male takes it over. The female returns to sea for a few days, but later shares incubation in equal shifts with her mate. Three incubation periods—of 38, 38 and 44 days—were obtained, the latter evidently due to snow-blockage, which lasted four days. At a single nest on Bird Island, South Georgia, Turner (1980) obtained a shorter incubation period of 35 days, and the chick subsequently flew to sea when 69 days old. Two fledging periods at Signy were determined at 65 and 71 days.

Only one chick was kept under close observation at Signy. When new-born it was covered with light grey down, but the facial area was bald; the eyes did not open until the ninth day—perhaps not surprisingly since the incubation period is so short. Apparently there was no initial twenty-four-hour brooding by the parents, as in other cool-climate storm petrels, but it was visited and fed each night and from a birthweight of 15g it put on weight rapidly, reaching 53g by the fourteenth day, and its maximum weight of 110g by the fiftieth day. Turner's chick at Bird Island followed the same regime, with no daytime brooding after hatching, and reached its maximum weight of 112g at sixty days. It then lost weight and was 81g on the day it departed. In one marked burrow at Signy the chick was trapped by autumn snow in April, and was finally entombed on the seventy-fourth day. 'Once the fledgeling has departed, the nest site is no longer visited by the adults. The population departs to lower latitudes, remaining absent from the islands (from May) until November,' state Beck and Brown. 'Failed breeders desert their nest sites soon after failure in February and March, and apparently leave the neighbourhood altogether.'

How far they migrate into tropical waters is not reliably known, owing to confusion with the more tropical *F. grallaria*; both species have been recorded north of the equator in the Indian Ocean, where Leach's petrel is notably numerous in the southern winter.

White-bellied Storm Petrel *Fregetta grallaria*

As already mentioned, this storm petrel is difficult to distinguish at sea from the black-bellied, both being the same size (19–22cm) and white on belly and under the wing, with dark head parts. In the hand, the entirely white under parts are distinctive. This petrel is temperate and sub-tropical in range, breeding on the Tristan da Cunha group in the Atlantic; on Lord Howe, Rapa and Kermadec (now rare) Islands in the western Pacific; on the eastern side on Juan Fernandez and some small islets off the Chilean coast; and possibly at Kerguelen. Wandering towards the equator in winter, it is

White-bellied storm petrels

known to Tristan islanders as the storm pigeon.

Comparatively little is known about its breeding habits, but its voice and the fact that it nests in burrows under tussock or thick grass, or under boulders, during the southern summer, suggest that it has only recently separated as a true species from the black-bellied storm petrel. Egg size and nestling colour are identical. At Lord Howe Island there is a dark race, almost entirely sooty-black. Murphy (1936) quotes Beck, who shot this species off Chile and recorded its mode of flight: 'Except when flying to windward, the feeding birds would use the leeward leg to maintain their momentum, kicking themselves into the breeze with this and holding the other leg stretched out behind.'

White-throated Storm Petrel *Nesofregetta fuliginosa*

This is a storm petrel of 21.6mm, with similar markings to the last two, but with a dark collar to the white throat; also it has a deeply forked tail and very long legs. It skips about with quivering wings when feeding at sea; like the last two it kicks off waves, but quite violently with a thrusting motion that gives the impetus for a long glide of approximately 20 to 30 seconds (Crossin, 1974).

It is confined to equatorial latitudes in the central and western Pacific, where it nests on the Line, Phoenix, Marquesas, Fiji and New Hebrides

White-throated storm petrels

Islands, chiefly on small islets that are free of rats and cats. In these tropical islands, the white-throated storm petrel has no fixed nesting period; the single egg has been found in almost every month of the year. There is obviously pressure to occupy the predator-free accommodation at any time, probably because this grows scarcer with increasing human interference, as we have all too often pointed out in this book. Crossin notes that in the tropical Pacific 'This seasonal spread of nesting apparently allows a greater number of birds to utilize the available nesting area than would be possible if nesting were limited to a specific time of the year for all individuals.' Conditions here resemble those on the Selvagens in the tropical north Atlantic (page 116): Bulwer's petrel *Bulweria bulwerii* occupies crevices or burrows on some white-throated storm petrel breeding islands (McKean is one) in large numbers; so does the abundant Audubon's shearwater *Puffinus l'herminieri*. The storm petrel uses these ready-made homes when they are vacated after the larger occupants have finished breeding. But they also use crevices too narrow for these competitors at any time of year.

Crossin is our authority for what little is known of the breeding of *Nesofregetta*. Nest sites were in existing cavities in the rocks or old fallen boundary walls, often on low islets in the sheltered waters of a coral lagoon, free of rats and the heavy Pacific swell; and usually further protected from the effect of direct sunlight by a screen of fringing grass (*Lepturus*). Little or no nest-lining is brought in, but the occupants may toy with feathers or twigs already present. Both birds are present for some days before the egg is laid, and at this time and during incubation a soft guttural groaning purr is uttered. In marked pairs incubation was shared. The egg is typical of a storm petrel, creamy-white with a prominent wreath of reddish and lavender dots about the large end: measurements of 20 eggs give an average of 37.95 × 27.45mm, relatively large for this small bird.

'The young hatch blind, but are profusely covered with medium-gray down. A chick estimated to be five days old had down to 20mm long on the back. I doubt if the young can use vision in the nest until they are in the large, fully feathered stage, since the entire orbital region is completely covered with shaggy down. When two-thirds grown they have a bi-colored aspect, brought about by the dark and light colored growth of new feathers beneath the down. It is not known how soon the young leave the island after attaining their juvenal plumage but apparently it is rather soon, as birds with traces of down still clinging to the feathers were attempting to fly at night.'

We find this normal in other fledgeling storm petrels. But Crossin observes an interesting trait in this storm petrel breeding on central Pacific islands. Here they have no diurnal avian predators, and he records that on

Audubon's shearwaters

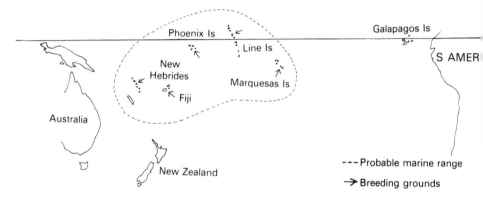

Breeding grounds and marine range of white-throated storm petrel

several occasions he saw adults arrive in full daylight to feed young. He remarks that such diurnal behaviour is 'never performed by any of the small hydrobatids in the eastern Pacific, since any individual showing itself during the day would be immediately set upon and devoured by Western gulls. The rapidity with which gulls attack storm petrels appears to be the sole reason why storm petrels never appear overland in daylight hours.'

However, in the eastern Pacific the Galapagos storm petrel *Oceanodroma tethys* (page 121), much smaller than the white-throated, actually flights home in daylight, being a nocturnal feeder like the resident gull *Creagrus furcatus*. Both are preyed upon by the resident *Asio* owl.

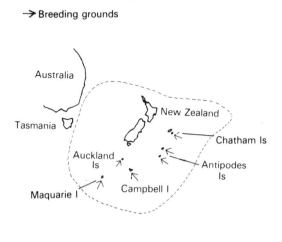

Breeding grounds and marine range of grey-backed storm petrel

Grey-backed Storm Petrel *Garrodia nereis*

One of the smallest storm petrels, 165–178mm, and identifiable at sea from the general grey appearance, with a black terminal band on the square tail. The breast is a duller grey, almost sooty, but below the breast the under parts are white, extending to the under-surface of the wings. Typically a southern ocean, cool-water species, nesting on the Falklands, South Georgia, Gough Island, Kerguelen, the Chathams, Antipodes and Auckland Islands. Its winter range does not seem to be extensive, but evidently it moves a thousand or so kilometres north from its cooler sub-Antarctic feeding and breeding area; it is present in the Hauraki Gulf, Northland, New Zealand, well out to sea, in August and September. The maximum number we have counted was 100 in a scattered group, feeding over a calm sea south of Little Barrier Island on 1 September 1981. They seemed more nimble and darting than the British storm petrel, but were keeping just as low, skimming rather than paddle-walking. They visit the Tasmanian coast but are not known to breed on the offshore islets there.

Limited studies at the burrows, said to be 'rathole-like', on small islands off the Chathams and Auckland Islands indicate that these are tunnels made in hummocks of old tussock, some within penguin and albatross colonies, and some mixed in with other storm petrel holes (notably those of thousands of white-faced storm petrels). The call has been variously described as a high-pitched twittering by birds flying above the nesting holes, or a creaking

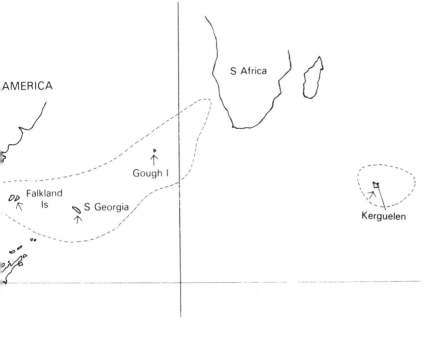

Grey-backed storm petrels

call like that of a crake. It is strictly nocturnal, and does not anywhere appear to be numerous. On the Antipodes, Warham & Bell (1979) saw individuals resting on the tussock at night frequently, January–March 1969, but found no nests or young. They comment: 'The lack of direct evidence for breeding is understandable, bearing in mind the dense vegetation, the bird's non-colonial nesting and its generally secretive behaviour.' Dense tussock and *Polystichum* ferns growing from old 'niggerheads', whose crowns of live and dead leaves are often interwoven intimately, make human walking tiring and time-consuming. Between these pillars the ground is a maze of narrow runways used by petrels and parakeets; 'Their activities in this super-terranean zone are almost impossible to observe, the pillars being so crowded together that birds may be heard but not seen.'

The breeding season extends from October to March. From February onwards on some of the islands the allied or little shearwater *Puffinus assimilis*, a winter breeder, takes over this tangled vegetation zone. As at the Selvagens already described, the breeding year is similarly shared on the Antipodes: two larger petrels make use of the larger burrows, the white-chinned petrel or shoemaker *Procellaria aequinoctialis* during the summer; and the pediunker or grey petrel *Procellaria cinerea* in the winter.

The nesting of the grey-backed storm petrel is probably typical of other small storm petrels. The single white egg with reddish dots at the blunt end averages 33 × 25mm (of 12 measured); incubation is shared.

Postscript

By an interesting but fitting coincidence on 4 March 1982, as I was completing the last chapter, which I begin with *Pelagodroma marina*, there was a telephone message from an Auckland housewife to say that, four days ago, she had picked up a pretty grey-and-white bird with webbed feet. It had struck a window one night, she had rescued it from the stalking cat, put it in an empty canary cage, and fed it bread and milk. Mrs Foot said she was worried about its future; it did not seem able to fly when released—it tried to, but only managed to run along the floor.

March is the month in New Zealand when the young white-faced storm petrel leaves its natal burrow, launching alone into the ocean with no better equipment than those long wings and legs, and an appetite and instinctive knowledge to enable it to survive.

How this fragile-looking Mother Carey's Chicken, just now sitting comfortably on my desk as I type, had taken the wrong direction and fallen among human well-wishers in an Auckland suburb, I cannot tell. But it had been calm at the time; perhaps heavy coastal mist had confused it if, as seems almost certain, the migrations of oceanic birds are guided by the moving sun and stars. From its new-looking plumage and clean unworn feet and toes, the webs almost transparent and but lightly tinged yellow in the centre, it is a fledgeling *P. marina*.

It has enjoyed a cleansing bath (I salted the water slightly—it will drink nothing but the sea or rain all its life) in our big laundry tub; and it accepted some fresh-shredded fish dipped in melted butter. It surely needs fat to keep its plumage waterproof; and in fact it has been demonstrating how it does this, by preening its feathers with that oily beak, which it uses at intervals to tweak the oil gland at the base of its tail.

There it sits, beady black eyes alert when I fidget, but half-closed when I am still. It even dozes, as if full-fed and of a mind to sleep. After this brief rest it wakes up fully, and begins to sway its head from side to side, looking downwards—most likely as it does in food-seeking at sea. It stands up easily on those long spindly black legs and three-toed webbed feet. It walks to the edge of the table, looks down, and takes off with long wings flapping; but can only flutter to the carpeted floor.

I pick it up and take some measurements: the wingspan is long—400mm;

the bill 20mm; the shank or tarsus 45mm; the centre toe with its soft flat claw 33mm. How beautiful is this morsel of sea-going life, perfectly adapted to wind and wave, restlessly wandering thousands of kilometres above the boundless ocean, through storm and calm! I am humbled by the little knowledge I have gathered and tried to set down in this book, discovering anew here, in my antipodean home half a world and fifty years away from that first joy of studying the Skokholm storm petrel, the wonder and admiration with which I first held one in my hand.

Look at the paper-thin webbing of the feet, just two panels stretched across three long toes (the hind toe is vestigial or absent in storm petrels)! The gannet has four toes holding three broad webs, with which it incubates by placing the foot on top of the egg—no brood patch develops in this large plunging sea bird. The gannet's nostrils are sealed externally to prevent water being forced into the mouth during the violent dive; but our little petrel has a conspicuous single tube on top of the bill which protects the nostrils within, the septum between not quite reaching the horny orifice. That single olfactory tube is now proved to be of vital importance—through it this little bird is able to collect and analyse odours at considerable distances at sea, especially edible oils and fat.

'Can you detect,' I ask it, as I set it down on my desk, 'the smell given off by masses of plankton at and near the surface, which is your principal food? I am beginning to think you can; some observers are suggesting you can smell your way from afar to your island home from the odours given off by hundreds of your storm petrel kin, and it is almost certain that your keen olfactory discrimination enables you to recognise the individual whiff of mate and child—and burrow? Perhaps you can even smell me?'

Already my study is scented with that powerful musky storm-petrel odour which, from long acquaintance, has for me a nostalgic inoffensive flavour. As if in reply, my guest begins again to wave its head from side to side. It is looking, and probably savouring odours, instinctively, or shall I say with childlike innocence—no 'malice aforethought'. It has already learned quite a lot from its contact with human hands: not to trust them, for it shrinks back when I lift mine towards it. It walks upright to the edge again, opens its wings and flutters to the floor. It defecates—a typical semi-liquid petrel squirt—on the carpet. (Lucky for me, I think, that so far it has not squirted warm stomach-oil at me—the usual reaction of healthy petrels towards enemies.) A good sign, indicating that it has taken nourishing food.

This time I replace it on my desk within a plastic ice-cream container so that it is not so easy for it to walk away, though for a while it restlessly tries to scramble over the edge. Presently it subsides, folds its very long wings so that the tips are crossed and extend, a black V, well beyond the tail. It ceases to sway its pretty head so inquisitively. During the time I have handled it, it has uttered a chittering protest, quite typical of most storm petrels when so disturbed, more or less identical with the hunger call of a chick when begging for food from a parent entering a burrow.

The cicadas keep up their late summer buzz in the camellias outside my study window, but inside there is silence as man and bird gaze at each other. The ruby-dark petrel eyes presently close as the handsome little head, with its white face set off by the black crown and elongated eye-patch, relaxes in sleep. Soundlessly I address this scrap of oceanic life, so unexpectedly my prisoner for a while:

'You seem so helpless, like some airy-fairy butterfly, here today and gone tomorrow, yet you will learn to ride out great gales at sea. How do you do this? Do you instinctively avoid them, or drift with them? Well are you named, *Pelagodroma marina*. At this very moment a cyclone is raging in the tropical zone north of New Zealand, which seems to be your normal wintering ground. The Tonga Islands are distressed, with many human homes destroyed. Get well soon, and as soon as you can fly properly, I will take you to Musick Point, a low cliff projecting into the sea near here, in sight of the Noisies islets, where you may have been born. I will set you free one evening when it is calm, and your land enemies, the gulls and visiting skuas in these waters, ought to be asleep; when the night sky is clear, and the stars are shining for you to steer by . . .'

The storm petrels
of the world

It will be noted that some species are quite unstudied, their life-histories little known, and even their breeding sites uncertain or imprecisely discovered.

Subspecies
We have tried to avoid naming and discussing geographical races, 'sibling' or subspecies of the species in this book. Although there is considerable variation of colour in some storm petrels, making subspecies of these variants is of doubtful validity, often in dispute, and frequently changing among taxonomists whose business it is to collect specimens and spend much time examining, measuring and assessing skins for museums. To list the subspecies they have named here would confuse the general reader, and greatly enlarge this book. We have therefore included below only those 21 storm petrels known to be true species—with distinctive characters developed in genetic isolation.

As a guide to body size, measurements are given—from tip of bill to centre of tail, with wingspan if known; plus a brief description of those species not already described in the previous chapters. In their generally accepted taxonomic order they comprise:

Wilson's Storm Petrel *Oceanites oceanicus*. See pages 137–54.
18–19cm (7–7.5in). Wingspan 41cm. Antarctic and southern ocean.

Graceful (Elliot's) Storm Petrel *Oceanites gracilis*. See pages 151–3.
15cm (5.8in). Galapagos Islands and coastal South America.

Grey-backed Storm Petrel *Garrodia nereis*. See pages 173–4.
16–19cm (6.5–7in). Sub-Antarctic oceans.

Frigate or White-faced Storm Petrel *Pelagodroma marina*. See pages 155–64.
20cm (8in). Wingspan 43cm. All southern temperate oceans.

White-bellied Storm Petrel *Fregetta grallaria*. See pages 168–9.
19–22cm (7.5–8.5in). Wingspan 48cm. Southern sub-tropical oceans.

Black-bellied Storm Petrel *Fregetta tropica*. See pages 164–8.
20cm (8in). Wingspan 48cm. Sub-Antarctic oceans.

White-throated Storm Petrel *Nesofregetta fuliginosa* (= *albigularis*). See pages 169–72.
21.5cm (8.5in). Wingspan 51cm. Tropical west and central Pacific.

Storm Petrel *Hydrobates pelagicus*. See pages 7–94.
14–19cm (5.5–7.5in). Wingspan 36cm. North Atlantic.

Least Storm Petrel *Halocyptena microsoma*.
14–15.2cm (5.5–6in). Smallest of all. Entirely sooty black, tail slightly wedge-shaped. Flight feeble and fluttering. Breeds on many small islands of the Gulf of California, wintering south to the Gulf of Panama in large numbers. Usually seen in sight of land, occasionally over 900km at sea off the coast of Mexico. About 15,000 birds nesting on the San Benito Islands in 1968. The single egg is laid in summer (May and June), well hidden in burrows in rock crevices, where scorpion, lizard and the curious fishing bat

Least storm petrels

N AMERICA

Baja California

--- Probable marine range

→ Breeding grounds

Pizonys vivesi also live. The bat is supposed to protect the petrel by eating scorpions and other insects, and to disturb the lizard which occasionally may eat a petrel egg or small chick. However, although a scorpion has been seen to carry away an egg when the sitting parent was removed by an observer, the curious association is maintained without serious predation. R. D. Ohmart, who observed the egg-thieving scorpion, thought that the fishing bat 'clumped with the storm petrel to avoid excessive heat and gulls, and possibly to gain in relative humidity' (Crossin, 1974). Compare the tiger snake and white-faced storm petrel co-existing in this way (page 158).

Galapagos Storm Petrel *Oceanodroma tethys*. See pages 122–4.
16.5–18cm (6.5–7in). Breeds on only a few islands in Galapagos.

Madeiran (Harcourt's) Storm Petrel *Oceanodroma castro*. See pages 114–22.
18–20cm (7–8in). Tropical Atlantic and Pacific oceans.

Leach's Storm Petrel *Oceanodroma leucorhoa*. See pages 95–113.
20–23cm (8–9in). Wingspan 48cm. Temperate north Pacific and Atlantic.

Guadalupe Storm Petrel *Oceanodroma macrodactyla*.
22cm (8.5in). Cannot be distinguished at sea from Leach's, but a somewhat darker bird, the white upper tail-coverts with dusky edges. This species may be extinct; it was last identified in 1911 at Guadalupe Island, which lies some 320km west from Baja California, Mexico. The situation at this island group is confused by the presence of both dark- and white-rumped races of Leach's storm petrel, some breeding in winter, others in summer.

Swinhoe's Storm Petrel *Oceanodroma monorhis*. See page 113.
18–19cm (7–7.5in). This and the next three species are all-dark, fork-tailed storm petrels, virtually impossible to distinguish at sea. This is the smallest, ranging south-west of Japan and the South China Sea, wandering to the north Indian Ocean. Nests on the Pescador Islands.

Matsudaira's Storm Petrel *Oceanodroma matsudairae*. See page 127.
25cm (10in). Large and fork-tailed.

Tristram's Storm Petrel *Oceanodroma tristrami*. See page 125.
23–25cm (9–10in). Wingspan 56cm. Large, all brown. Deeply forked tail.

Markham's Storm Petrel *Oceanodroma markhami*. See page 134.
23–25cm (9–10in). Wingspan 56cm. Indistinguishable at sea from Tristram's.

Hornby's Storm Petrel *Oceanodroma hornbyi*. See page 136.
20–23cm (8–9in). West coast of South America.

Ashy Storm Petrel *Oceanodroma homochroa*. See page 124.
19cm (7.5in). All dark, but larger than the least petrel, and confined to breeding farther north along the outer coast of California.

Fork-tailed Storm Petrel *Oceanodroma furcata*. See pages 128–34.
20cm (8in). Wingspan 45.5cm. Cold and temperate North Pacific.

Black storm petrel

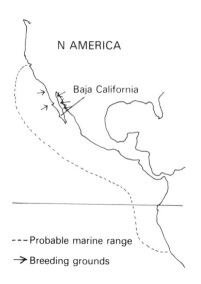

Black Storm Petrel *Loomelania melania.*

23cm (9in). One of the largest of the all-dark storm petrels, with deeply forked tail; until recently placed in the *Oceanodroma* genus. Breeds on small islets inside and outside the Gulf of California, and winters as far south as the Gulf of Panama. Its breeding biology seems to be close to that of the British (European) storm petrel: courtship in May, egg laid in June, fledging in the autumn. The call has been described as 'puck, puckaroo' on the wing, and typical twittering from nest cavities. These are under boulders, making a study of banded birds difficult, but giving protection from predatory birds. It is sometimes found nesting in the same rocky cavities as the least petrel. Strictly nocturnal, and often found fatally impaled by night upon the spines of the cholla cactus *Opuntia.*

Predators and parasites

The recorded heavy predation by diurnal gulls and skuas is evidently a principal reason for the nocturnal visits of storm petrels to their breeding grounds where these enemies exist. Despite this predation, and that suffered from the attacks of owls, hawks and, more rarely, snakes, scorpions, crabs and lizards, the numbers of storm petrels breeding in the world seem to be well maintained, even increasing, at least on those islands, and a few mainland sites, where there are no other significant predators. These colonies, however, cannot survive the introduction and continued presence of large rats—the Norwegian *Rattus norvegicus*, the black or ship *R. rattus*, and the small Polynesian *R. exulans*—except on sheer cliffs where rats, cats and mustelids are unable to reach the petrel nesting holes.

External parasites

Like all warm-blooded animals, storm petrels may be host to ectoparasites which cling to the body, upon which they feed, and are transported throughout the range of the species. Most of these are host-specific, rarely found except on the animal they parasitise; in particular body lice may never voluntarily leave the host, and some, such as those that live on the human body, have become specialised and specifically distinct to reside on certain warmer or safer parts of the host's surface. Thus five species of feather lice (*Mallophaga*) live from egg to adult upon the body of the Manx shearwater, inhabiting variously the wings (a long thin-bodied louse concealing itself by clinging to the feather shafts, making preening more difficult), the neck and the head (a stout squat type adapted to cling to the short feathers which cannot be preened by the bill, but only be the front claw). Little work has been done on the several species of feather lice recorded from storm-petrel species in different latitudes. As *Mallophaga* do not normally suck blood, but feed on down, feather and skin scale debris, they do not much affect the health of oceanic birds, and are probably at their lowest numbers on their host during the long period of the bird's sea-wandering. They are likely to be most numerous during the nesting period, when in the warmth of the burrow the louse-egg, which is cemented to a feather close to the shaft, hatches within a few days of being laid, and the perfect young louse will be able to infest the growing petrel chick, thus ensuring its food supply.

Bird fleas (*Aphaniptera*), derived comparatively recently from mammal fleas, are less specialised; most of them are host-specific, but if by accident parted therefrom can survive temporarily on other birds and mammals, including man. Fleas suck blood during their adult life which is spent clinging to their host; but drop their eggs in the warmth of their hosts' homes. Here the larval grub hatches and lives on the organic debris of the nest, including the droppings of the adult fleas which contain residues of undigested host-blood. It then pupates in a silken cocoon. When the adults and young birds leave at the end of summer, the nest may be alive with fleas of all ages; but fleas do not like cold, and unless the bird-flea can find an alternative warm-blooded host, all the adults become moribund and die, leaving only the eggs and cocooned larvae to survive the winter in hibernation. The warmth and movement of the bird returning to breed next season triggers the young fleas into activity. It is believed that few fleas survive on the bodies of sea birds which are absent from the land for most of the year.

On Skokholm a curious burrow-breeding flea situation existed during my time there. The Manx shearwater has only one specific flea, which we called the Joyful One, from its scientific name *Ornithopsylla laetitiae*. This flea was occasionally found on the storm petrels which nested in small side-burrows within the more labyrinthine shearwater colonies. Also it was recorded from burrows inhabited by the numerous puffins and rabbits on both Skokholm and the neighbouring island of Skomer. The curious situation was that, although the rabbit's specific flea *Spilopsyllus cuniculi* is numerous on the neighbouring island of Skomer, only 4km to the north, it was quite absent from Skokholm. This is the more inexplicable because: (1) I had more than once introduced some fresh rabbit blood to improve the rather small race inhabiting my island, by bringing in some of the larger (flea-infested) mainland and Skomer Island rabbits; (2) these importations had been a regular improvement measure in the past, according to rabbit-trappers who exploited the Skokholm crop before I came to live there; and (3) there was a frequent interchange of small numbers of sea birds—gulls, puffins, shearwaters and storm petrels (as proved by banding records)—between the two islands which could have accidentally transported rabbit fleas from one to the other. The puffin, for instance, is highly popular with fleas, six species having been recorded from it, including the rabbit flea.

Fleas can convey the virus of several lethal diseases, transferring it when biting a healthy animal after sucking the blood of one affected by the disease. When Sir Charles Martin was investigating for the Australian Government the possibility of using the virus disease of myxomatosis to control the plague of rabbits on that island continent, he offered to get rid of the rabbits on Skokholm. From an experiment in which this virus, introduced in a small colony of rabbits enclosed at a research station at Cambridge, induced the disease and killed every rabbit, he supposed the disease was spread by body contact. Mistakenly (as I now think) I agreed to a trial at Skokholm, as at that time (1936) I was anxious to get rid of the wild rabbits in favour of more profitable sheep. Details of what was thought would be a 'safe' experiment on our isolated island, preliminary to the possible release of the lethal myxoma virus in Australia, are given in my book *The Island*. Suffice it to say here that the introduction of the virus had no effect on the population of rabbits on Skokholm; only the deliberately inoculated rabbits died.

Subsequently, when myxomatosis reached Britain from France in 1955, it gradually spread and at last reached Skomer, evidently carried by infected fleas which had climbed aboard gulls or other predatory birds returning to roost on the island after feeding on infected mainland rabbits. The virus killed about 99 per cent of the rabbits on Skomer, where the disease still recurs with each recovery from an epidemic—as on the opposite mainland. But it has never reached Skokholm, for the very good reason that there are no rabbit fleas, now proved to be the essential vector in Britain of the myxoma virus.

By comparison with other island nature reserves, Skokholm seems to be remarkably free of fleas and ground-living ectoparasites of birds, although no satisfactory explanation has been forthcoming. Theoretically it might be that the notably very high ant population on Skokholm carries off the eggs and cocoons of the fleas during the long winter resting period; also, it has been suggested, the swarming autumn population of hungry house mice could be responsible in the same way, exploring for every source of food when their normal vegetarian diet of grass and herbs shrivels before the early winter gales. Finally the rabbits themselves may be indirectly responsible; they too are hard put, and numbers die of malnutrition like the mice, when the grass, overgrazed during the late summer, is nibbled down to the roots. The resulting seasonal bareness does not provide much cover for parasites which overwinter in soil and vegetation.

Probably for the same reasons blood-sucking ticks and mites, which can cause serious loss of blood to small birds, are comparatively rare on Skokholm, although reported in large numbers on other storm-petrel islands, including Skomer.

Internal parasites

It is impossible here to list the numerous microscopic protozoan parasites, including virus and coccidia, some of which cause diseases in sea birds; or the flukes, round- and flat-worms which require intermediary hosts for the completion of their life-cycle—'an odyssey compared with which the voyages of Ulysses seem singularly uneventful', to quote Rothschild and Clay in their *Fleas, Flukes and Cuckoos* (1953). In any case, hardly anything is known about the species and degree of infestation of storm petrels by these internal parasites, which vary in size from less than a pinhead to worms longer than the petrel itself. The stomachs of many marine animals, from albatrosses and smaller petrels to whales, often contain hundreds of worms, sometimes in a writhing ball. These are largely derived from their fish prey; most of them do not greatly, if at all, affect the health of the host, in whose guts some of them mature, and from which their spent bodies and ripe eggs are voided. The worm eggs are swallowed by fish, and the cycle begins again with the hatching of the eggs and the penetration and growth of the early stage of the worm within the tissue of the fish.

It is unusual, perhaps unique, for an internal parasite to cause the death of a bird which it is not known to inhabit. But D. Claugher (1976), by a nice piece of research, put together such a true story. New Zealand Wildlife Service scientist Don Merton reported finding on South-east Island in the Chathams that, of hundreds of thousands of six species of petrels which breed there, only 2 per cent of those examined were free of an anklet or shackle of fibrous material. In particular, over the whole of this island of 216 hectares, he found that the most abundant species was the principal victim. At approximately one to two square metre intervals, one white-faced storm petrel, *Pelagodroma marina*, lay shackled and dead—out of a total estimated population of at least one million pairs (page 163).

If this mortality estimate is approximately correct then the dead represented 10 per cent of the white-fronted storm petrels on this island in one season, from just this unusual cause only; add to this the heavy predation by skuas and gulls on the island, and the mortality seems well nigh unsupportable.

Examining 120 specimens of the euphasid crustacean (a krill shrimp) *Nematocelis megalops* in the British Museum (Natural History) which had been collected on the Challenger Expedition, Claugher found that 90 per cent were parasitised by the larval form of the trematode worm *Distomum filiferum*. Only two of these infected shrimps had two worms, the other shrimps had only one parasite: 'Filaments were found protruding outwards and downwards on each side of the crustacean, between the carapace and the first abdominal segments. In some cases the filaments appeared to trail from one of them, usually on the left side of the crustacean.' These filaments are both elastic and sticky in water, and can be stretched well over one hundred times the length of the host shrimp! Free-swimming in this elongated form, the larval worm seeks contact with its second intermediary host—a fish. As soon as it does so, the wriggling animal attaches itself by means of anterior spines, casts off its tail, bores into its fish host, and feeds on its tissues. Later it becomes an encapsulated metacercaria or cyst before it emerges as a mature tailless fluke, able to lay eggs within the host's body by self-fertilisation. These eggs are voided and eaten by the *Nematocelis* shrimp as they float in the sea; and the cycle begins afresh.

Fortunately, although millions of these eggs must be eaten as part of the planktonic food of whales and sea birds, they apparently do not develop in the bodies of other than the krill shrimp. It is while the larval worm is free-swimming after it leaves the host shrimp that the unfortunate storm petrels, their feet dangling as they dip their heads to pick up their plankton food, tangle their legs with the sticky larvae which embrace and shackle them. On return to their nesting grounds, the petrels gradually become incapable of walking, as the fibrous material hardens around their legs. They can no longer mate, incubate or feed their chick. Hence the mortality recorded by Don Merton. In this shackled state many are easy victims of skuas and gulls; and no doubt small storm petrels on other islands in the seas where the shrimp host of *Distomum filiferum* is parasitised in this way, must suffer a similar mortality.

Yet, surprisingly, the heavy mortality from this cause does not seem to have had any noticeable effect in reducing the breeding population of the white-faced storm petrel. Those who have lately (1982) visited South-east Island and know it well, tell us that this lethal shackling of storm-petrel legs, although it occurs every summer, is less severe in some years, when the larval parasite is evidently less numerous.

It is a true saying that predator and parasite need to live in equilibrium with their prey if both are to survive. But it is difficult to see what benefit the worm parasite derives from this accidental association with and transportation by a bird which results in the extinction of both!

Bibliography and
Acknowledgements

Ainley, D. G. 1980. *Auk* 97:837–53
Ainslie, J. A. & Atkinson, R. 1937. *British Birds* 30:234–48
Ardley, R. A. B. 1936. *Discovery Report* 12:349–76
Bannerman, D. A. 1959. *Birds of the British Isles*, Vol 8
Beck, J. R. & Brown, D. W. 1972. British Antarctic Survey Scientific Report 69
Billings, S. M. 1968. *Auk* 85:36–43
Boersma, P. D. & Wheelwright, N. T. 1979. *Condor* 81:157–65
Brothers, N. P. 1981. *Corella* 5:29–33
Claugher, D. 1976. *Journ Nat Hist* 10:633–41
Cramp, S. et al. 1977. *Handbook of the Birds of Europe, the Middle East and North Africa*, Vol 1
Crossin, R. S. 1974. 'The Storm Petrels'. Smithsonian *Contrib Zoology* 158:154–205
Davis, P. 1957. *British Birds* 50:85–101 & 371–84
Fisher, J. & Lockley, R. M. 1954. *Sea-birds of the North Atlantic*
Furness, R. W. & Baillie, S. R. 1981. *Ringing and Migration*
Gill, R. Jr. 1977. *Auk* 385–6
Gross, W. A. O. 1935. *Auk* 52:382–99
Harris, M. P. 1969. *Proc California Academy Sciences* 37:95–166
Huntington, C. E. 1963. *Proc I O Congress* 13:701–5
—— & Burrt, E. H. 1972. *Proc I O Congress* 15:653
Hutchison, L. V. & Wenzel, B. M. 1980. *Condor* 82:314–19
Imber, M. J. 1975. *Notornis* 22:302–6
—— 1976. *Condor* 78:366–89
Johnson, A. W. 1965. *Birds of Chile & Adjacent Regions*, Vol 1
Lambert, K. 1971. *Beitz, Vogelkund* 17:1–32
Lockley, R. M. 1932. *British Birds* 25:206–11
—— 1942. *Shearwaters*
Mainwood, A. R. 1976. *Ringing & Migration* 1:98–104
—— 1978. *Ringers' Bulletin* 5:33–4. Also unpublished
Murphy, R. C. 1936. *Oceanic Birds of South America*, Vol 2
Palmer, R. S. 1962. *Handbook of North American Birds*
Richdale, L. E. 1943. *Trans Roy Soc NZ* 73:97–115
Roberts, B. B. 1940. *Brit Graham Land Exp 1934/37*, *Sci Rep* 1:141–94
Salomonsen, F. 1967. *Biol Medd DanskeVid Selskab* 24(1):1–42
Scott, D. A. 1970. 'Breeding Biology of Storm Petrel' (Ms DPhil:c660, Oxford University)
Serventy, D. L. *Proc IOC* 14:165–90
Simon, T. R. 1981. *Auk* 98:145–58
Stonehouse, B. 1960. *Wideawake Island*
Van Oordt, G. J. & Kruijt, J. P. 1953. *Ibis* 615–37

Warham, J. & Bell, B. D. 1979. *Notornis* 26:121–69
Wilbur, H. M. 1969. *Auk* 86:433–42
Yapp, W. B. 1970. *The Life and Organisation of Birds*
Zink, R. R. & Eldridge, J. L. 1981. *British Birds* 73:385–7

The author wishes to acknowledge with thanks and pleasure the assistance he has derived from many ornithologists interested in these smallest of oceanic birds: in particular the work of, and in several cases the personal discussions with, the authors of the books and papers listed in the Bibliography.

Also, his warmest thanks to Noel Cusa for his collaboration, expert knowledge and skill in portraying the subtle differences in plumages of storm petrel species; and for his considerable help in reading the text.

Index

Numbers in **bold** type refer to illustrations